# FAMILY THREADS

## A Family Memoir in Quilts

### Lisa Krenz

# FAMILY THREADS

## *A Family Memoir in Quilts*

Copyright © 2017 Lisa Krenz

All rights reserved. No part of this publication may be reproduced, stored in any retrieval system, or transmitted in any form or by any means, mechanical, photocopying, recording, or otherwise, without permission in writing from the publisher, except by a reviewer, who may quote brief passages in a review.

Cover and interior design by Ted Ruybal at www.wisdomhousebooks.com

Manufactured in the United States of America.

ISBN 13: 978-0-692-85069-5
CRA031000 CRAFTS & HOBBIES / Quilts & Quilting

1 2 3 4 5 6 7 8 9 10

# TABLE OF CONTENTS

Introduction . . . . . . . . . . . . . . . . . . . . . . . . . . . . . . . . . . . . . . . . . . . . . . . v
Why Quilts . . . . . . . . . . . . . . . . . . . . . . . . . . . . . . . . . . . . . . . . . . . . . . 1
A Starting Place . . . . . . . . . . . . . . . . . . . . . . . . . . . . . . . . . . . . . . . . . 7
The Koester Grandparents . . . . . . . . . . . . . . . . . . . . . . . . . . . . . . . 13
Buried Treasure in a Cardboard Box . . . . . . . . . . . . . . . . . . . . . . . 21
Setting up Housekeeping . . . . . . . . . . . . . . . . . . . . . . . . . . . . . . . . 41
Wedding Quilts . . . . . . . . . . . . . . . . . . . . . . . . . . . . . . . . . . . . . . . 49
For the Love of Children and Grandchildren . . . . . . . . . . . . . . . . . 57
Another Very Special Gift . . . . . . . . . . . . . . . . . . . . . . . . . . . . . . . 69
The Aunt Hilda Quilts . . . . . . . . . . . . . . . . . . . . . . . . . . . . . . . . . . 73
Inheritances . . . . . . . . . . . . . . . . . . . . . . . . . . . . . . . . . . . . . . . . . 83
The Embroidered Quilts . . . . . . . . . . . . . . . . . . . . . . . . . . . . . . . . 89
Quilts and our Church . . . . . . . . . . . . . . . . . . . . . . . . . . . . . . . . 101
Quilting Heyday of the 1980s & 90s . . . . . . . . . . . . . . . . . . . . . . 109
Barn Quilts—an Old Quilt Idea for the New Century . . . . . . . . . 121
The Quilts Continue . . . . . . . . . . . . . . . . . . . . . . . . . . . . . . . . . . 125
The Cast of Quilters . . . . . . . . . . . . . . . . . . . . . . . . . . . . . . . . . . 135
Postscript: Now It's Your Turn . . . . . . . . . . . . . . . . . . . . . . . . . . 139

# INTRODUCTION

## I come from a long line of aunts.

Aunt Norma, Aunt Bernadine, Aunt Ruby, Aunt Flo, Aunt Mary. And my aunts had aunts: Aunt Anna, Aunt Hilda, Aunt Bertha, Aunt Louise, Aunt Lydie, Aunt Sophie. My mother is an aunt. My cousins all call her Aunt Jean, and they always say it with a big smile. Growing up, I didn't always know who some of the great aunts were or how we were related, but it didn't matter; if someone had the word 'aunt' in front of their name, that meant an automatic kindness in both directions. You're my aunt, we're connected and that's good.

Being an aunt is different than being a mother; it allows for a certain freedom and affection not afforded mothers and daughters. Sometimes we listen to our aunts in a way that we won't listen to our mothers. Perhaps aunts are more lenient with nieces and nephews than with their own children. If an aunt spoils a niece or nephew, they aren't to blame for the child's bratty behavior. Maybe it's a little like being a grandparent, but it happens when you're younger and you get to enjoy it longer. An aunt can take the time to teach a niece or nephew something and focus on just that one thing. An aunt doesn't have to worry about teaching the child to be responsible, or pay for their college, or make sure they get a job. In the end, though, the things you learn from an aunt

Family Threads: A Family Memoir in Quilts

or uncle often go beyond the narrow task at hand. Often we learn things from these special relatives that last a lifetime.

Koester siblings: Aunt Ruby, Aunt Bernadine, Uncle Glenn, Jean, Aunt Flo at Aunt Bernadine's 50th wedding anniversary in 2001.

Ruby with her Aunts Bertha, Lydie, and Leona, taken in the 1960s at Carol's confirmation.

I had the great fortune to spend six or seven weeks during most of my childhood summers throughout the 1970s visiting my relatives in Southern Illinois. Most kids go off to camp for the summer, but not me. I went to the farm in Southern Illinois. Each of my mother's sisters would take me to live as part of their family for a week, sometimes two, as would my mother's brother and his family. The uncles were all there, of course, but they generally didn't inhabit the kitchens and everyday activities of the household like the aunts. Aunt Flo did not live on a farm, although she did grow up on one. She and her family lived in town, but it was a very different type of town than the suburb I was used to. I wouldn't trade my farm/small town 'summer camp' for anything.

## Introduction

My Liefer cousins at Aunt Ruby's farm, probably 1966 or 1967
L-R: Donna (baby), Carol, me, Ronnie, and Janel.

These summer visits are some of the happiest memories of my childhood. I learned about chickens and cows, tractors and gardens, baking cookies and eating watermelon out of the garden. I even got to use an old outhouse at my grandpa's. He had installed an indoor bathroom somewhere around 1968, but the outhouse had to be experienced. Together with cousins we explored dusty attics and barns, chicken houses and milk houses, field roads and corn fields. Suburban girl goes to the country, nothing could have been better.

One might think that I would miss my mother being away from her for so long, but that rarely happened. Not because I didn't love my mother but because a part of my mother was in each aunt. Little parts of her were with me wherever I went. My aunts and uncles or my grandpa would share memories and stories of her with minimal prompting. When we'd go somewhere and run into non-relatives or more distant cousins, the conversation often went something like this, "Oh, you're Jeanette's daughter! Look at you. How is your mother? I heard she went all the way to Colorado. My goodness. Oh, I remember your mother..." I especially loved it when they said, "You're Jeannette's daughter." It made me feel so proud. Being an only child is lonely sometimes, but when I was with the aunts and uncles and cousins I was connected to something bigger, something that stretched back for generations. I was part of the Koester and Hartmann clans and that was no small number and no small thing.

During that decade of the 1970s, my aunts and uncles were all younger than

I am now and were busy raising families and making a living. They all seemed very wise and strong and tall. During those childhood summers I learned some very practical skills: baking, sewing, water skiing (thanks to Uncle Glenn), the fine art of making mud pies, embroidery, the care of chickens, how to navigate a dairy barn, how to walk barefoot on a rock road or through a cow patty, and the list goes on. Many of these skills I continue to employ to this day, well . . . not the ones related to rock roads and cow patties. Even more valuable than learning these specific skills, I learned about what it means to work hard, love your family, serve your neighbor, and live your faith.

A visit to Aunt Ruby at her farm, 1985.

I don't remember my aunts quilting during those 1970s summers. They were too busy with young families and summer chores, but all their beds were covered with quilts. Quilting was as much a part of these women's lives as baking a pie or tending the garden. Not everyone enjoyed these tasks, but they knew how to do them. Each house had a sewing machine—some were used more than others, but everyone had one. My Grandma Koester passed away in 1965, but even in my grandfather's kitchen, Grandma's old treadle sewing machine rested under the window, long since retired, but remaining as a physical reminder of her place in our family.

## Introduction

Eventually I got older and spending the summer with the relatives didn't coordinate so well with summer jobs and teenage activities. Then there was college and career. Growing up didn't mean that I lost touch with my relatives. It just meant I didn't get to see them as often or spend unbounded summer days with my cousins, but those relationships were solidly quilted into the fabric of my being. Moving to St. Louis in 1989 meant that I could finally be close for all kinds of events and regular visits. This is when the quilting stage of my life really began in earnest. Women in my family had been quilting for generations, but I never paid much attention to it until I was an adult. When in the early 1990s my interest in quilting was awakened, I knew exactly where to turn to learn this fine art: my aunts. My first quilting lessons started with Aunt Ruby and a box of my leftover sewing scraps, and I haven't stopped yet. I quickly discovered that making a quilt was so much more satisfying than sewing a dress or a skirt that never seemed to fit just right. A homemade quilt held much more intrinsic value than a homemade pair of pajamas and lasted much, much longer.

Family history and genealogy is a popular pastime, but rarely when you're young. It's not until we ripen for a while longer that we appreciate the value of such documentation. Several years ago, a distant cousin, Margie Buch (on another trunk of the Koester family tree) compiled an extensive genealogy book documenting our family back to the early 1800s. Remarkable in its complexity and detail, I am happy to have this record, but I must admit it leaves me wanting something more, something visual, something that gives me a tangible sense of who these people are. A document of such magnitude is too epic to imagine, but the idea has led me in another family history direction. I've always enjoyed history and so, too, my quilting interests have often led me in historical directions. While reading books about quilt history, it dawned on me that my very own relatives had beautiful quilts in their possession. Perhaps our family's stories could be told through their quilts. I knew I had several quilts that my aunts had made for me, and I suspected that my aunts had quilts that they had received from their aunts, and so on. When I approached my aunts about this project they were all very happy to share their quilts with me, but none of them had ever considered that their quilts were out of the ordinary—not that they didn't consider any of their quilts special to them, but we aren't ones to toot our own horns.

These quilts are special. They are special because they are connected by the threads of our family. They are interesting in their artistry and in their practicality as well as how they fit into a greater picture of history. This isn't a complete listing of all the quilts in the extended Koester/Hartmann-related family, but it does cover approximately a century's worth of women and their quilts.

A single thread on its own isn't worth much, but a single thread is exactly what's needed to start piecing together a block or quilt a line across the sandwich of fabric and batting to hold it all together. You can only make a quilt one thread at a time. Put several strands of thread together, one after the other, with color, design, and love—then you have something both beautiful and powerful. Throughout the pages of this collection you'll see the threads of our family story told through the quilts of some of the women who our family comprises. It's certainly not the whole story, that would be impossible, but I hope it gives us a glimpse of who we are and who we've come from so the next generations may know who they can be.

# WHY QUILTS

Asking why we have quilters in our family seems akin to asking, why do we have farmers in our family? I don't know; it has just always been. It wasn't something anyone ever talked about that I remember; it just was. We are a practical people, first and foremost. Back in the 1800s when our ancestors came from Germany, they wanted to eat and make a living so they found a corner of Southern Illinois with good land, planted seeds, and raised livestock. They needed bedding to keep warm at night, so they made quilts. When you have a lot of children you needed a lot of quilts. Some in my family still farm, some still make quilts. Many do neither. Maybe it's like inheriting green eyes or that crooked little toe. Maybe there's a gene for farming. Maybe there's a gene for quilting. I don't know. If so, over the generations those traits have expressed themselves in some and not others. Never any judgments. Just part of our living history.

There is also a cultural component paired with the practical component. Handwork, or stitching, is a skill that all young girls learned well into the 1970s. I learned to embroider from my mother and my aunts when I was young. It was something that all girls just knew. By my generation it wasn't really a necessity, more like a vestige of an earlier habit. Not so long before my time, if you needed something in your household or farm, very often you made it yourself. Aunt Ruby tells me that it takes four plain feed sacks to make a bed sheet, and growing up all their sheets were made this way, as were their undergarments.

## Family Threads: A Family Memoir in Quilts

Working on the farm in the 1940s—everyone pitches in.

L-R: Florence (later my Aunt Flo), their dad Bill Koester (my grandpa), Glenn (later my Uncle Glenn) and Jeannette (my mother).

All my aunts had sewing machines in their houses; it was just part of the necessary furnishings of a house in mid-20th century middle America. Even my mother, the career woman, started her married life in 1963 with a sewing machine, a trusty blue Singer model that I wish I still had. She never learned to quilt but she could embroider and learned those skills right along with her sisters.

On the farm a person never just sat and did nothing. If you were sitting and working on embroidery (I contend that embroidery might just be the gateway drug to quilting) you were doing something worthwhile. Everyone had embroidered pillow cases, dresser scarves, tea towels, and doilies. Some enjoyed the handwork; others didn't and gave it up as soon as possible. Some took up crochet or the making of clothing.

I also have a sneaking suspicion that in the days before television, giving young girls stitching to work on was a way to keep them occupied and out from under a busy mother's feet. It gave girls something productive to do while watching cows in the pasture or passing winter hours stuck in the house. To our modern ears it sounds like sexist gender roles forced on girls at a young age. Maybe it had something to do with little girls' propensity for better fine motor skills and sitting still longer than boys. I sincerely doubt anyone ever gave it any sociological thought at the time.

## Why quilts?

I think it had more to do with simple division of labor. Someone had to know how to sew on buttons, turn a collar when it was worn, or repair a torn shirt. Someone else, usually the boys, had to repair machines and build fences. Lest you get an idyllic picture of early 20th century farm girls merely sitting and stitching their days away, I'll remind you that just because girls were learning to sew doesn't mean that many weren't also milking cows, driving tractors, feeding chickens, and tending gardens. They could do both. In fact, perhaps the sewing was a chance to rest and do something creative.

Aunt Flo tells that the reason Great Aunt Hilda quilted so much more than Flo's mother, my grandmother Ella, was because Hilda had some kind of ailment and the doctor had told her to sit and rest more. Hilda followed doctor's orders by sitting and working on quilts. Ella seemed never to sit, always working hard to help on the farm or prepare food in the kitchen. Ella also didn't have a place in her house to put-in (the term for putting a quilt in a large quilt frame) a quilt since the Koester grandparents were in residence in the front room for close to a decade, then later Uncle Albert. She would, however, go to Hilda's house and quilt with her sister, a time to be together and still be doing something productive.

We also are very fond of making quilts and giving them to those we love. I doubt this is unique to our family. For generations we have given quilts for all of life's big milestones: weddings, babies, graduations, and anniversaries. Sometimes we give quilts to help a new wife set up a household of her own. Sometimes we receive a quilt as a remembrance or thank you from someone dear to us. The quilt maker may have gone on to heaven but their stitches, their loving care, remain in the tangible form of that particular quilt.

Another integral part of our family's lives has always been the Lutheran church. There was a time, not so long ago, that every Lutheran church in Southern Illinois had a ladies' group that quilted to raise money for their church and for missions. Many of my aunts have quilted with women's groups from their church, as have I. It's a way to serve the Lord and visit with our friends at the same time. I've gotten to know such wonderful women through our quilting group at church that I wouldn't have gotten to know otherwise. It's a unique connection when you've all stitched on the same quilt together. I'm sure my aunts would say the same.

Quilting is no one's primary focus in my family. No one in my family makes a living, or any income for that matter, from quilting. We no longer need to make our own bedding and haven't had to for quite some time. I've noticed that a strong interest in quilting seems to skip around generations. It doesn't always get passed directly from mother to daughter, but often passes from aunt to niece. Most of us who do quilt have gone long stretches without working on a quilt, especially when our children are young and our households are teeming with activity. As I collected the photos and information about our family quilts, I noticed a trend of more quilting activity when children get older and begin to leave home, which leaves larger open spaces in life for quilting. In our family timeline of quilting

Detail of back corner of doll quilt.

## Why quilts?

we've moved past the age of quilting as necessity and into the age of quilting as creative and giving outlet. For me, the desire to be creative and to give to others is just as necessary. Perhaps it's a necessity that's been there all along.

One of the first quilts I remember is this small doll quilt that had been my mother's. As an eight- or nine-year old child I found it folded in the bottom of my mother's sewing box and quickly appropriated it as my own to wrap my treasured doll in her cradle. I knew even then that when you loved something (or someone) you wrapped it in a quilt.

This 22" x 14" quilt was machine pieced with ¾" half-square triangles and no batting inside. It was made by mother's grandmother, Johanna Rowald Hartmann (born 12/2/1874, died 7/26/1965—mother to Ella, Anna, Ernst and Hilda). It's obviously a scrap quilt and was likely made in the 1940s since my mother was born in 1941. Grandma Hartmann also made one for my mother's sister, Flo, and her cousin, Lorene (Hilda's daughter), probably all at the same time. Aunt Flo says she remembers that her grandma put their initials on the back so that the girls could play together with their dolls without mixing up their quilts. In the photo you can see the letter "J" for Jeanette, embroidered on the back. The remarkably small scrap pieces give testament to the fact that our foremothers never wasted anything. Grandma Hartmann was not known to be a 'fancy' quilter, typically making more plain quilts with a purpose. I love the use of the lights and darks in this quilt and would hardly call it plain. This one has no batting and is backed with basic muslin, perhaps a basic feed sack of some kind. We have no relics of my mother's childhood. She was the fifth daughter in a family of six children; saving keepsakes was frivolity, so this doll quilt is indeed a treasure to me. Maybe this first quilt experience has something to do with my lifelong love of scrap quilts.

Family Threads: A Family Memoir in Quilts

There's not just one simple answer to the question as to why we have all these quilts in our family, but when you boil it all down, we are a practical people who love each other very much. At the intersection of those qualities I've found a great big pile of quilts, a tangible legacy of that love and sturdiness.

Grandma Hartmann with some of her grandchildren
L-R: Lorene Koester, Florence Koester, Grandma Hartmann, Jeannette Koester, Leonard Koester.
Grandma Hartmann made doll quilts for these three granddaughters.

# A STARTING PLACE

In my mind the trunk of our family tree is planted in a farmhouse built by my grandfather, William (Bill) Koester, about 1920 or thereabouts on a plot of land across the Kaskaskia River from the small town of Evansville, Illinois, population 300, give or take a few here and there. His plot was meager. If this were a proper genealogy I should start in the generations before my grandfather with the first immigrant from Germany, Carl W. Koester, who was born in Germany in 1806 and came to Randolph County, Illinois, in 1836. Since someone has already done that, and done a marvelous job of it, I'll not repeat that gargantuan feat.

No, this is more of a family sampler quilt. I think of my grandfather's white clapboard farmhouse, and those that lived in it, as the center medallion of our story. The irony is that not many quilts were pieced in that house and few, if any, were actually quilted there, but it seems as if we are all connected by the people that once lived in that place.

On October 24, 1920, Bill Koester married Frieda Nagel when he was 26 years old and she was 22 years old. They lived in that white clapboard farmhouse with the two parallel front doors that opened onto a small square of a front porch that reached out like a small dock into the yard. The house sat close to the

Bill Koester and new bride Frieda Nagel—wedding photo, October 24, 1920.

Bill and Frieda Koester circa 1920.

road without a long lane like some farms, but instead had a drive that circled to the side of the house and around in front of the milk house and the barn and the machine shed. Bill would live and farm the rest of his life in this circle of buildings that sat close to the Kaskaskia River, which often flooded and crept threateningly close to the house and often blocked the road to town.

Frieda gave birth to their first child, Norma, on January 23, 1926, and their second daughter, Bernadine on April 19, 1929. Their third child, Ruby, was born on April 11, 1933. It must have been a difficult pregnancy as they hired Ella Hartmann from nearby Percy to help with the housework and caring for the children. Sadly, Frieda passed away from complications of the pregnancy on May 5, 1933. Bill and Frieda's wedding photo with its round frame and curved glass hung in the front room of the farmhouse ever after.

In the 1930s it was unheard of for a man to care for a newborn infant, so Frieda's sister, Bertha, who was married to Bill's brother, Charlie, took baby Ruby home to care for her. Ruby would stay with her Aunt Bertha and Uncle Charlie

## A Starting Place

Aunt Bertha and Uncle Charlie at their anniversary—these flowers were most likely the altar flowers from church to celebrate their anniversary.

and their two teenage daughters, Leona and Valeda, until Ruby was about eighteen-twenty four months old. Ruby and her Aunt Bertha remained close throughout the rest of their lives. Later, Ruby and her husband Norbert would build their farmhouse on adjacent land to Bertha and Charlie in Prairie (rural Red Bud), Illinois. In their older years, after their granddaughter had moved into the home place, Bertha and Charlie lived in a small house at the end of Ruby and Norbert's lane. While Ruby was a primarily self-taught quilter, she credits Bertha as being her main teacher. This special relationship was forged very early and remained strong even until today, as evidenced by the quilt that Ruby still owns, this Dresden Plate, sometimes called Sunflower, made by Aunt Bertha.

We rarely know the whole story of a person's life. When you're a younger member of the family this is particularly true. Elder members of the family seem to have always been old and it's difficult to imagine them when they were young, difficult to imagine their story before they were what they are to you now. We meet them at a certain age and only really know them from the experiences we have with them from that point on. It means we just naturally miss out on the parts that came before us. Quilts can be that way, too. But like so many relatives of ours who are older, this quilt had a rich and meaningful life long before my arrival.

Dresden Plate or Sunflower quilt made by Aunt Bertha, now owned by Aunt Ruby.

I first met this quilt as a child on my summer visits to the farm in the 1970s and it resided on Aunt Ruby's bed. I had no idea it was already decades old and had already led a full life. Like any other kid, it never occurred to me to ask about its pattern or provenance. I just remember laying across the cool cotton on hot summer afternoons, inspecting the various pretty fabrics. I had no idea that each piece had been traced and cut out carefully by hand. Aunt Ruby says she just 'wore it out' with use over the years.

It wasn't until we started this project that I learned more of the story behind this quilt. This Dresden Plate quilt was likely made in the late 1930s or very early 1940s. It's a classic example of a thirties scrap quilt in color and form and the use of the black stitching to outline the plates and the scallop. Ruby suspects the fabrics had all been bought at Schrieber's Store in Red Bud and were probably mostly scraps from dressmaking. The Dresden Plate blocks demonstrate a highly skilled quilter, but even more remarkable is the intricate border using the same pieces as the blocks but all fitting together masterfully into graceful scallops echoing the blocks. The blocks and border are all highlighted by the black embroidered buttonhole stitch. It measures 80"x79", with the blocks measuring 15-½"-16". The hand quilting still holds it all together even after so many pieces of the 'plates' have worn away.

## A Starting Place

The quilt maker, Bertha Nagel Koester (b. 1891, d. 1971), married Charles Koester in 1914. She was sister to Frieda Nagel who had married Charles's brother, Bill, in 1920. She was an accomplished seamstress. By the 1940s, she was in her fifties. Her children were grown and married and she was not yet a grandma. One can only speculate as to why she made this remarkable quilt. I wonder if she was as impressed with it as I am. Perhaps she was just using up her scrap pile, as so many quilters do. I can only imagine that she had more time and creative inclination to tackle such an intensive project, just like many of us increase our quilting at a similar age and period in our lives.

This is not, however, the entire story. How did Bertha's niece, Ruby, come to have the quilt on her bed all those years later? We have to go back to the farmhouse that Bill Koester built to answer that question.

Up-close look at the corner of this quilt including a block and the detailed border.

# THE KOESTER GRANDPARENTS

In the time after Frieda's death in 1933, Ella Hartmann, who had originally been hired as a housekeeper during Frieda's pregnancy, stayed on to keep house and help care for Bill's young daughters, Norma and Bernadine. By June 1st of 1934, she and Bill were married. She was 35 years old and Bill was 40 years old with three young daughters. A Hartmann family history written in the late 1970s states: *"Ella did housework for different families. One day Wm. and Frieda Koester ask her to come work for them until their third child is born. After child birth and Frieda died, she must have felt sorry for Wm. so she stayed on and married him and raise his three children and had three of her own and the children hardly knew they were step children. They lived on a farm all their married life."* Ella's younger sister, Hilda Hartmann (b. 1913) married Bill's younger brother Walter (b. 1908) a month later, on July 29, 1934. Once more, two sisters were married to two Koester brothers. Hilda and Walter lived just down the road, a few miles from Ella and Bill on the original Koester home place. Their youngest son, Floyd, lives there still today. Glenn Koester, Bill and Ella's only son and youngest child, continues to live in the farm house his father built in 1920.

Indeed, Bill and Ella went on to have three more children, Florence, born

Koester Family Photo circa mid-late 1950s
Top row L-R: Norma, Jeanette, Florence, Bernadine, Ruby.
Front row L-R: Bill (their dad), Glenn, Ella (their mom).

in 1938, Jeanette, born in 1941, and Glenn born in 1945. I can't speak to the part of the quote about Ella feeling sorry for Bill; had never heard that before, but I do know that she loved all the children as if she had borne them all herself. There was never any talk of being step-sisters or half-sisters. They were all sisters and brother and that was that. Growing up, I knew that my grandpa had had a wife that died and she had been mother to Norma, Bernadine, and Ruby. I only knew this because Frieda's picture was still in the front room and because there were Nagel relatives that were still part of the family circle, not because of any negative comments about being half-related in any sense.

Back to the story of the Dresden Plate quilt.

For about eight years, starting in the early 1940s, Grandma and Grandpa Koester (Carl b. 1864, d. 1949 and Wilhelmina b. 1867, d. 1951) lived with their son Bill and daughter-in-law Ella Koester and their children, Norma, Bernadine, Ruby, Florence (Flo), and Jeannette (Jean). This was a very common practice during this time and Bill and Ella had five daughters to help with such care. Since Jean would have just been a toddler and Flo still quite young when they first arrived, I'm not sure how much help they were. Glenn was born during the time that

## The Koester Grandparents

Ruby Koester marries Norbert Liefer
May 4, 1952.

Grandma and Grandpa Koester were in residence. Since Ella already had a full house and no extra time to quilt, she wouldn't have had extra bedding on hand for one more bed. Bertha, now her sister-in-law, gave Ella the Dresden Plate quilt to use for Grandma and Grandpa Koester's (Bertha's in-laws, too) bed. The Dresden Plate was, no doubt, not a quilt made quickly. It seems safe to assume that Bertha already had this finished and was maybe even using it in her own home when she saw the need that her sister-in-law Ella might have for it in housing the elderly grandparents. My guess is that she was not worried about its return, that she was just doing her part to care for family.

After the Koester grandparents had both passed away, (Grandma Koester died in 1951), Aunt Bertha said that Ruby should take the quilt. Ruby was married the next year and used it on her own bed for many years until, as Ruby said, she just 'wore it out'. By the time I first remember the quilt in the 1970s, completely unbeknownst to me, it had already lived a long and dutiful life.

Ella and Bill set up a bed in the front bedroom for the Koester grandparents, since all the other rooms in the house were full and going up the stairs to the attic would have been impossible. This room also held the baby crib for whichever small child still needed it. Later, their Grandpa Koester's bachelor brother, Uncle Albert, would come to live with them and take up residence in the

Bill Koester and his second bride, Ella Hartmann (my grandparents) wedding photo June 1, 1934.

living room. The kitchen was likely already the main room and gathering place for the family, but now there was definitely no extra room anywhere just for sitting and relaxing. I'm told that Ella rarely sat anyway and certainly no one living on a farm saw relaxing as a necessity. It's hard to imagine all those people under one roof, with no indoor plumbing and no electricity until the late 1940s. I didn't know my grandmother, Ella, since she passed away in 1965 when I was just a year old, but I understand from every family member I've ever talked to that she had a very caring and loving personality so she would have been a natural to take on the overwhelming task of caring for elderly in-laws. I'm told that Bill, my grandpa, would also have been quick to agree to take on such a task. Walter (Bill's youngest brother) and Hilda lived down the road and my mother says she remembers Hilda bringing trays of ice cubes to their farm in the summer since Hilda and Walter had electricity much earlier than did Bill and Ella. Walter and Hilda also shared produce from their garden and meat at butchering time to help support the Koester grandparents. Walter was also always quick to come over to help when Grandpa Koester's dementia caused him to wander off down the road to town. My mother remembers speaking 'low' German at home because that was the language that the grandparents spoke. Later, after Grandpa Koester was gone, Uncle Albert moved in and took up

## The Koester Grandparents

Bernadine Koester marries Otis Wegener
June 6, 1951.

The Koester Grandparents (Carl and Wilhelmina) Lived with Bill and Ella and children. This snapshot appears to be from an anniversary celebration (hence the fancy cake) and is taken in the front room of Bill and Ella's house, probably during the time that they lived there.

residence in the living room. Bernadine told of Grandma Koester passing away May 24, 1951, just two weeks before Bernadine's wedding on June 6, 1951, so in a short time there was a funeral and a wedding all in the same family.

Even though Ella had quilted when she lived at home, as evidenced by the orphan blocks (see the next section) that we have from the period before 1934, once she took over the Koester household there was no longer time or space for such an endeavor. Even though her treadle sewing machine was a permanent fixture in the kitchen, no one remembers Ella working on quilts at home. She was known, however, to go to Hilda's house to quilt with her sister.

Even though we have no quilts from Ella, the Dresden Plate quilt is not the only quilt from this time period. Ella and Bill's daughter Flo has this Shoofly quilt in her collection now. Flo remembers that her grandmother was 'housebound' during her later years, the late 1940s and into 1950 and '51. Flo would have been 10 to 13 years old and remembers ironing the scraps in this quilt

# Family Threads: A Family Memoir in Quilts

Shoo-Fly quilt made by Grandma Koester during the time she lived with her son and daughter-in-law, Bill and Ella Koester.

Detail of individual Shoo-Fly block.

for her grandmother to piece into blocks by hand. Even though Grandma Koester couldn't move much, she could still deftly use her needle to piece this useful and lovely quilt. I hope when I can do little else, I will still be able to piece a quilt. Perhaps Ella helped her set it all together with the sewing machine. The fabrics appear to be primarily sewing scraps in various plaids and shades of blue, possibly fabrics from shirts and everyday work clothing from the family. Even though it uses scraps, it still has the artful element of the blue inner border with white muslin setting blocks and outer border, all set together on point. It is visually quite pleasing. Since there was no room at Ella and Bill's to put a quilt into a large frame for quilting, this quilt was most likely quilted at Aunt Hilda's by Hilda and Ella and whoever joined them for quilting.

Decades later, Flo's husband, Carl, had a 1947 Plymouth that he often showed at antique car shows. They would display this quilt across the back seat since the two were from the same time period.

Consider the woman whose fingers pieced these blocks, Wilhelmina Dierks Koester, was born just after the Civil War in 1867 and passed away during the Korean War in 1951 and even today, in yet a third century, we can still hold in our own hands evidence of her creative energy. Even into her last years when perhaps her strength and abilities were limited, she was able to contribute to her family through the making of this quilt.

Family Threads: A Family Memoir in Quilts

Carl Koester and Wilhelmina Dierks
(Grandpa and Grandma Koester)
Wedding photo—April 6, 1887.

Koester family, likely taken in the late 1950s. Back row—Ruby, Norma, Bernadine, Glenn, Flo and Jean. Front row—Ella and Bill.

# BURIED TREASURE IN A CARDBOARD BOX

## THE QUILT CATALOGUE / ORPHAN BLOCK

Buried treasure comes in all different forms. For me it was a dented cardboard box full of quilt blocks waiting patiently undisturbed for decades. While I was in the process of collecting quilt pictures and stories for this project, Aunt Flo brought me a shallow cardboard box full of sample blocks. She said something along the lines of, "Lorene (Hilda's daughter) and I found these when we were getting ready for Aunt Anna's sale back in 1993. Aunt Hilda said we should keep them. We always wanted to do something with them but just didn't. Maybe you might be able to do something with them?" Maybe?!

Aunt Flo estimated that the Hartmann sisters, Ella (b. 1899), Anna (b. 1904), and Hilda (b. 1913) had worked on most of these more than sixty blocks when they were all still living at home before they married in the early 1930s. The sisters grew up with their brother, Ernst, in rural Percy. Their father, Christian Hartmann, worked at a flour mill in Steeleville for over forty years. The Hartmann family history records that he walked the one mile to work, and in all those years only missed one day of work due to hip-high snow that had turned to ice.

The Hartmann siblings-late 19teens
Anna, Ernst, Ella Hilda in front.

Unpacking these blocks, I found meticulously hand-pieced blocks, some better constructed than others, as well as machine-pieced blocks. The fabric in these blocks appears to date from the 1890s through the early 1930s, as well as some that must have been added much later in the 1950s by whoever was in possession of the blocks. Ella was born in 1899. Just as quilters today often have fabric in their stash for years, so, too, it would have been common for dressmaking scraps to remain in or be recycled through the family 'scrap bag' for a decade or more. While the use of feed sack fabric became very popular in the 1920s and 1930s and for years after, the majority of the fabrics in these blocks are likely not feed sacks, but sewing remnants. The dark navies, blacks, and claret reds are quite indicative of the decades surrounding the turn of the 20th century. Cadet blue became very popular as synthetic dyes became cheaper following WW I. Other common colors of this time period are the double pinks, cheddar, and gold. During this time period most dark fabrics have small-scale designs in white or one color; notice, too, the frequent use of the 'shirting' fabric, small, dark designs or stripes on a white background. It's not until the late 1920s and early thirties that new fabric dying technologies made it possible to easily print fabrics with more colors and more white in the background.

The fabrics in the Grandmother's Flower Garden block are perfect examples of the change of fabric by the 1930s. The Log Cabin block also features lighter pastels and feed sack muslins with some of the shirtings from earlier blocks. Notice the change in the shade of the reds from a wine-colored red to a brighter red in the newer blocks. Thanks to changing technologies, colors become more colorfast and stable by the 1930s.

The varying sizes and colors of these blocks indicate that they were never intended to be assembled into one quilt; most likely they were blocks made as patterns or samples. These collections were often called a "Quilt Catalogue" or "Orphan Blocks". While some newspapers ran columns that printed quilt patterns and mail order patterns were available, the best way to get and keep a new pattern was to make a sample from a friend's quilt.

Log cabin Block pattern.

Most of the blocks are hand pieced, but not all. Notice the two versions of the basket block. Another common practice was to take a block from a worn-out quilt and save it as a pattern. You can see the newer, brighter red block on the right next to the faded block with the shadows of old quilting still outlining the pieces. Many of these blocks are difficult to make with curved pieces, diamonds, and half-square triangles. We don't know if these patterns found their way into completed quilts, as I am not aware of any quilts from this time period that we have in our family. These blocks would have been made by tracing each piece from a cardboard template, cutting the pieces individually and then sewing them carefully together by hand, a far more time-intensive process than today's rotary cutter and speed-sewing methods.

I have no way of knowing who pieced which blocks, exactly when they were made, or the origins of the wonderful fabrics. I can only imagine what these sisters talked about over the making of these blocks when they were young, unmarried women. Born in 1904, Hilda was the youngest by 9 years and went on to be a very prolific quilter. She may not, however, have had much to do with most of the blocks in this collection because of how young she was at the time most of them were made. I wonder if she might have made the last three blocks pictured, the fabrics of which seem to date from a later period, probably the 1950s. I believe Hilda likely made hundreds of quilts over the course of her lifetime, some that are documented here. She taught her daughter Lorene and her niece Flo to quilt. I have very affectionate memories of both Aunt Hilda and Aunt Anna, but my grandmother, Ella, was the eldest and passed away in 1965 when I was only a year old. Since she did not quilt in her home while raising children, these blocks are the only quilting legacy we have of her.

While Aunt Anna seems to have worked on these blocks and had a number of quilts from this time period at her estate auction, she is not remembered as someone who liked to quilt later in life. It was at her estate auction in the early 1990s that I really got excited about antique quilts. Unfortunately, at the time I did not have the financial means to acquire any of her quilts, but other family members did. My cousin Marlen's wife, Karen Liefer (Norma Koester Liefer's daughter-in-law),

Anna and Ella—probably around the time that the orphan blocks were being made, late 19teens.

## Buried Treasure in a Cardboard Box— The Quilt Catalogue / Orphan Block

# Family Threads: A Family Memoir in Quilts

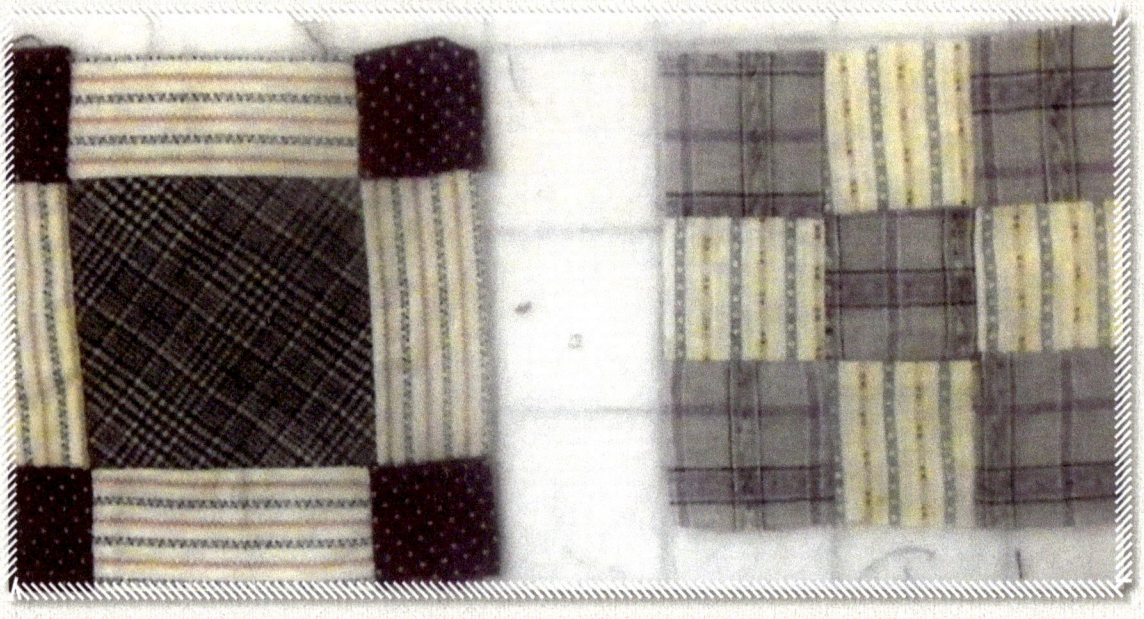

Buried Treasure in a Cardboard Box— The Quilt Catalogue / Orphan Block

Family Threads: A Family Memoir in Quilts

Buried Treasure in a Cardboard Box— The Quilt Catalogue / Orphan Block

# Family Threads: A Family Memoir in Quilts

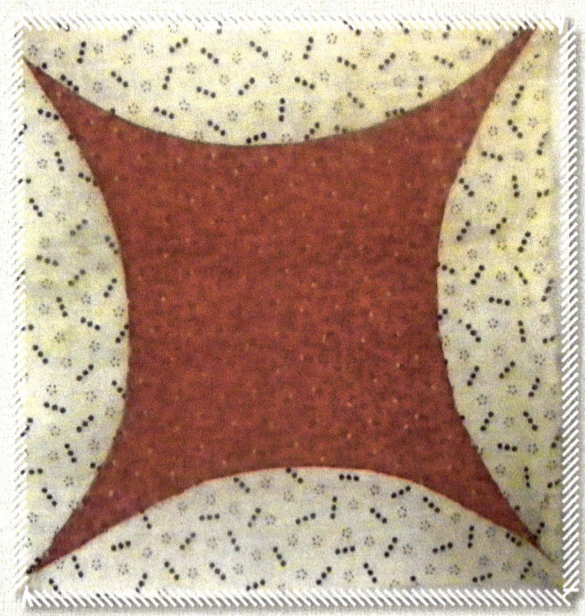

Buried Treasure in a Cardboard Box— The Quilt Catalogue / Orphan Block

Family Threads: A Family Memoir in Quilts

Buried Treasure in a Cardboard Box— The Quilt Catalogue / Orphan Block

# Family Threads: A Family Memoir in Quilts

## Buried Treasure in a Cardboard Box— The Quilt Catalogue / Orphan Block

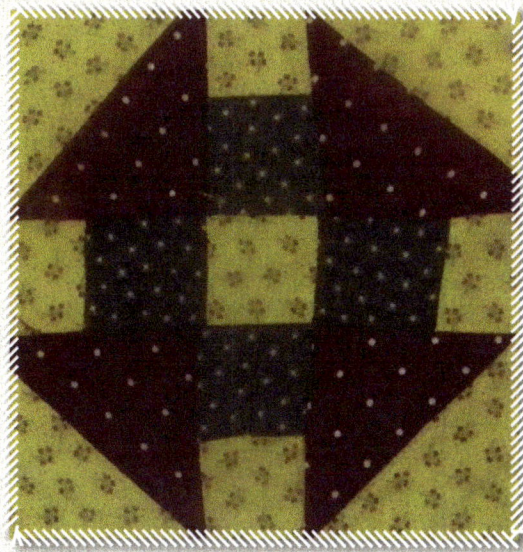

35

# Family Threads: A Family Memoir in Quilts

Buried Treasure in a Cardboard Box— The Quilt Catalogue / Orphan Block

Family Threads: A Family Memoir in Quilts

was fortunate enough to acquire a quilt made by Aunt Anna at her estate auction. It is a scrappy, nine-patch quilt, measuring 78"x80". The blocks measure 4 ½" and are very neatly set together on point with bubblegum pink (very indicative of this time period) gingham setting squares. It has an inner border of cream shirting fabric with the gingham for the outer border. The nine-patch blocks are made primarily from plaid shirting fabric plus a few dress or feed sack prints, but the pink yardage appears by its quantity to have been bought for this quilt. Pencil markings for the quilt designs are still very clear and dark, and the quilt appears never to have been washed. The top is machine pieced and the quilting is done by hand, with very thin cotton batting, if any. Maybe this was made to be a summer quilt. The quilting is done by hand but is very simple in design. We assume that Anna made it since it was on her auction, but we have no way of knowing for sure without a signature to validate its maker.

Family Threads: A Family Memoir in Quilts

It would seem unusual for a gift to be made of scraps unless made by a sister. Anna married Ralph Erle on June 22, 1930. Perhaps Anna made this quilt in the early years of her marriage and never found a use for it. Anna and Ralph never had any children so she had no need to cover so many beds. They lived on a farm just on the edge of Red Bud. Ralph also worked at a car dealership for 25 years, for eight of which he owned the dealership. They had the financial means to buy store-bought bedding, and perhaps she preferred the more fashionable ready-made bedspreads. Ralph and Anna traveled extensively in their retirement years and perhaps the quilting bug just never infected her.

The women who made these orphan blocks have gone on to heaven. The clothes whence they were carved and the people who wore them are long gone, but the blocks remain, stitched together by sisters' hands. Those hands once held each other and later held our growing hands, all so very long ago, but with these blocks they continue to reach toward us and teach us today.

Anna Hartmann and Ralph Erle-wedding photo, June 22, 1930.

# SETTING UP HOUSEKEEPING

Bedding is essential to the starting of a new home, especially since we spend about a third of our lives sleeping or in bed. It's a private, intimate place, our beds, yet it is also a public space to display something beautiful. Typically the bed and its covering are central to the bedroom and its décor. That expanse of cloth that warms and protects us also sets the psychological tone for the room.

In generations past, women would spend time as young girls and teenagers preparing for their future role as keeper of the home. To the modern young woman the whole concept of a 'hope chest' sounds sexist and like something out of a *Little House on the Prairie* novel or from the days of the Depression, but we're really only a few generations away from such a practice, the tangible evidence of which still remains in the possession of our family members. Whether we practice the old-fashioned practice of preparing a hope chest or not, getting married and starting a new household are still milestones in a family's life and thus we mark them by the making of quilts. This will never go out of fashion.

Flo (Koester) Zschiegner has just such a hope chest product in her collection. Flo's mother-in-law, Helen Rathert Zschiegner, made this embroidered dove quilt for her hope chest before she married Max Zschiegner in Red Bud in 1921. It measures 78 ½" x 78 ½" and is hand embroidered in light blue, hand pieced, and hand quilted. The workmanship is remarkable. There are 81 identical dove blocks in a 9x9 configuration. Helen and her husband became missionaries to China and served there from 1921 to 1940. She would have taken this quilt with her to China in the 1920s. It is in very good condition for having traveled so far.

The embroidered dove quilt by Helen Zschiegner.

Detail of dove block.

Decades later, in the 1950s Helen's son, Max Zschiegner (brother to Flo's husband Carl), became a missionary to Japan. Of course, being a man, he had no hope chest for which to bring home goods. Helen sent this Hexagon quilt along with him, saying it was 'used,' so it would be good to take along to Japan. Max's wife, Taka, gave it back to Flo many years after their time in Japan. Since Helen had returned from China in 1940 and Max went to Japan in the 1950s, it was likely made in the 1940s or early 1950s. The quilt measures 79" x 82" and is hand-pieced and hand-quilted. This quilt is an excellent example of a feed sack quilt and has a wide variety of fabric samples. Some of the fabrics may have also been scraps of aprons and dresses. There are not many fabric repeats. To our modern eye it seems quite remarkable, but in the eyes of its

## Setting up Housekeeping

Helen Zschiegner's hexagon quilt.

Detail of hexagon blocks.

maker, Helen Zschiegner, it was just an 'everyday' quilt, nothing special so it would be good to risk on such a faraway journey.

Flo was also the recipient of two 'setting up housekeeping' types of quilts in the early years of her marriage. The first, and older of the two, was a simple nine-patch in shades of gold and white from Aunt Anna. The 75½" x 79" machine-pieced and hand-quilted quilt was already used when Anna Hartmann Erle gave it to her niece, Flo. Flo and Carl were married on May 11, 1958, and this quilt appears to have been made maybe even a decade before. Anna seems to favor the 'on point' arrangement of the nine-patch blocks as she used a similar setting in the nine-patch that we have of hers from the 1930s. Flo said she was in need of bedding for her new home in Red Bud and Aunt Anna gave her this one for that purpose. If you hold it up now, you can practically see through it, it has been so well used.

Flo has another nine-patch intended for a similar purpose but with a different color palette. This brightly colored nine-patch quilt top, set together with white sashing and cornerstone blocks, was made by Flo's Aunt Selma when Flo was first married. Aunt Selma gave it to her, so Flo would have something for her bed. Aunt Selma was married to Ernst Hartmann who was brother to Ella (mother to Flo), Anna, and Hilda. Aunt Selma and Uncle Ernst lived in the Percy/Steeleville area at the time. Selma was known as quite a good seamstress but had no children of her own. Flo and Aunt Hilda (Selma's sister-in-law) quilted it at Hilda's farm in rural Evansville. Flo remarked when showing me this quilt that she remembers Aunt Hilda being upset that some of the white squares had been pieced together from two smaller pieces of white. I suppose if you were making a quilt top for someone as a gift, it wasn't acceptable to be quite that frugal. The 76" x 86" quilt is machine pieced and hand quilted with 7-½" blocks. This quilt

Nine patch in gold and white.

Detail of nine patch block.

Patchwork ninepatch.

was likely pieced around the time Flo was married in 1958. Flo and Hilda quilted it in 1958/59. The scraps were likely from feed sacks and sewing scraps.

Many years later when I was just learning to quilt, my first quilt was a similar nine-patch made from sewing scraps. The changes in fabric colors between the 1950s and the 1990s are obvious. I pieced this quilt from sewing scraps in 1993 under the tutelage of Aunt Ruby. Aunt Ruby said that a nine-patch was the best block to start learning with and made a cardboard square and showed me how to use it to trace each square for cutting into the pieces to make the nine-patch block. Once we had traced and cut enough squares to get started, she showed me how to sew them together in proper order. Eventually, I traced every square for this quilt and cut each one out with a scissors. Even though the rotary cutter had long been invented by this time, Aunt Ruby was not using one, and still isn't. It wasn't until a year or two after this that I took a class at a local quilt shop and discovered the joys of the rotary cutter. I started calling this my "quilt of my twenties" because I was using fabrics that were all accumulated during the decade of my twenties. I finished this quilt just as I was turning 30 years old. Most were sewing scraps but some were crafty-type scraps. The bubblegum pink and white stripe pieces came from a house dress of my paternal grandmother (Agnes McLaughlin) who had recently passed away. Some of the sewing scraps came from clothes I had made in college and some from my early teaching days. Thus the fabrics seemed to represent all that I had been doing during the decade of my twenties.

I was not savvy then to mathematical issues related to using half-square triangles and quarter-square triangles and the need to make them bigger to leave room for seam allowances, so almost all the corners are cut off on the outside edge of the nine-patch portion of the quilt.

Once it had been pieced, Aunt Ruby found a quilt frame for me that didn't

## Family Threads: A Family Memoir in Quilts

Detail of nine patch blocks.

sell at an estate auction. She then put new fabric on it for me (actually, I suspect Uncle Norbert did that) and brought it to me in St. Louis. Ruby and Flo helped me set up the frame and get the quilt in the frame, then stayed and quilted a while to get me started. There's no way I could have managed any of that on my own. I still have trouble getting a quilt in a frame. If you look at the stitches in this quilt, it's very obvious which are Ruby and Flo's stitches and which are mine. Mine are enormous and quite uneven. If I recall correctly, they came across the river (from Red Bud to St. Louis) once or twice more to help me quilt on this quilt. It took me about six months to finish quilting this on my own.

## Setting up Housekeeping

After making this quilt, I was hooked on quilting and rarely made clothes for myself again. Quilts were much more fun and always fit just right. This quilt, however, didn't turn out to be the best quilt for 'setting up housekeeping'. I hadn't planned very well and it was too small for a double bed and looked too feminine. Later when my daughter (Anna, born in 1999) was old enough for a 'big girl bed' she used this quilt on her twin sized bed intermittently for about ten years, alternating it between this one in summer and another, sturdier quilt I'd made just for her, in winter. Now, twenty years after its making, it shows considerable wear on the binding edge and the batting has thinned out quite a bit after numerous washings.

My first Nine Patch quilt, 1993-1994.

Family Threads: A Family Memoir in Quilts

Me quilting.

# WEDDING QUILTS

The practice of making quilts and bedding and such for one's 'hope chest' is long past, but the practice of giving quilts for weddings has been going on for centuries and I suspect will continue for as long as people make quilts and get married. Sometimes entire quilt shows are based around wedding quilts. There is even a quilt named the Double Wedding Ring. It is a very difficult quilt to piece and we have none in our family's collection that I know of. The Double Wedding Ring quilt isn't the only pattern that can be given for a wedding. In fact, in our family, quilts with embroidered blocks seem to be a popular wedding gift choice.

Donna Buch Wegener is the owner of two beautiful embroidered block quilts that she received as wedding gifts from her mother, Ruth Buch, and her mother-in-law, Bernadine Koester Wegener.

The first quilt here was made by Bernadine Wegener (b. 1929) for her eldest son Richard's wedding in 1974. She let her soon-to-be daughter-in-law, Donna, choose the colors. Notice that there are 12 embroidered blocks in this quilt rather than the standard six, resulting in a rather unique setting. Bernadine embroidered the blocks and had the quilt hand-quilted by the Ladies Aid of St. Peter's Lutheran Church in Evansville, Illinios, a group that Bernadine has been quilting with for decades. Notice also the prairie points as the binding of the quilt. This was very popular by the 1970s and continues to be a popular, although time-consuming, choice. Bernadine made wedding quilts for all of her children's weddings; this was just the only one that was available for photographing.

Donna's mother also made her a quilt for her wedding, since she, too, was a quilter. Ruth Buch (b. 1925, d. 1978) made a quilt for each of her children for their weddings. Donna said that she picked the colors for this quilt and embroidered the blocks herself. Her mother set it together and most likely had the Ladies Aid quilters of Trinity Lutheran in Prairie, Illinois, quilt it for her. It, too, has the prairie points as the binding. This large star pattern is commonly used for setting together embroidered blocks, but the use of the half-square triangles around the center block is more unusual. The backing is purple to match the blocks on the front. By this time in the 1970s, the use of polyester high-loft batting was very popular. It is easier to quilt and shows off the intricate quilting designs very well.

Bernadine's wedding gift to her son and new daughter-in-law.

Detail of block.

Wedding gift to Donna and Richard from Donna's mother Ruth Buch.

## Wedding Quilts

Richard Wegener (Bernadine's oldest son) marries Donna Buch—April 26, 1975.

On my wedding day with Aunt Flo and Uncle Carl. Lisa McLaughlin and Stephen Krenz Wedding day—July 1, 1995.

Flo also made a quilt for her daughter, Bev, when she got married and set up housekeeping. Flo made this embroidered quilt for her daughter and son-in-law, Bev and Steve Gruenwald, in 1992, after they had been married several years to supplement the other quilts that she had made Bev. Notice how she alternates the six embroidered blocks with blank blocks that had matching quilting to make a nine-patch arrangement. Flo embroidered the blocks, set it together, and quilted it at home with help from her Aunt Hilda and sister Ruby.

It's not just mothers and mothers-in-law who continue the quilt as wedding gift tradition. Aunts frequently give quilts as wedding gifts, a most generous and loving gesture. Aunt Flo, my baptismal sponsor, gave me this embroidered quilt for my wedding in 1995. I was very surprised as I did not know that she had been making this for me. Aunt Flo made quilts for all her godchildren on the occasion of their weddings. This quilt has six embroidered blocks that Flo embroidered and set together with this interesting chevron pattern. She hand-quilted it herself, probably with the occasional help of her sisters.

The stitches are very tiny and uniform. The fabrics are green and mauve, a very popular color combination in the late 1980s and early 1990s.

Aunt Ruby also had established the practice of giving nieces quilts for their weddings, but when I moved to St. Louis in the early 1990s and began expressing my enthusiasm for quilts, it appeared as if I might not be getting married any time soon. I had my own single-girl apartment, then a house, so I had certainly set up housekeeping, but without benefit of the wedding gifts. During this time I was teaching full time and working on my master's degree so had not yet started making quilts myself. On one particular visit in 1992 I had been admiring the unique pattern of the Log Cabin quilt on Ruby's bed, how the dark parts of the blocks formed two hearts. Ruby suggested I bring my box of sewing scraps down to her house and we could see about finding enough leftovers for a Log Cabin quilt, even though I had no prospects for getting married any time soon. It wasn't long before I made another visit with a package of 100% cotton batting because the top was finished. I can't remember where she

Flo's gift to her daughter Bev.

Wedding gift to me from Aunt Flo.

## Wedding Quilts

Detail of Log Cabin blocks.

found the backing, but it was something she had already, probably a sheet, light mauve to coordinate with the border. She quilted the whole thing very quickly, in just a matter of months.

Having this homemade quilt from Aunt Ruby remains a treasure to me. I often wondered if she made it because she thought there was no hope of me marrying or if she just wanted to encourage my love of quilting. Either way, the next year (1993) when I finished my master's degree, I promptly went for another visit to Aunt Ruby's with my scrap box under my arm again, but this time to learn to piece my very own first quilt, the nine-patch shown earlier in this section. For my wedding in 1995, we received some very lovely embroidered pillow cases stitched by Aunt Ruby to match this quilt. We still use this quilt on our bed, especially in the spring and summer.

Aunt Flo has undoubtedly been the maker and giver of innumerable quilts. For her fiftieth wedding anniversary she was the recipient of a quilt to

# Family Threads: A Family Memoir in Quilts

Log Cabin quilt. Made by Aunt Ruby with my sewing scraps, 1992.

mark that special occasion. Lisa Kloepper (the quilter of this quilt) has been a friend and neighbor of Flo for years and years, at least since their children were little, back in the early 1960s. Lisa embroidered these purchased blocks and pieced the quilt to give Flo and Carl for their fiftieth wedding anniversary in May of 2008. She enlisted the ladies from St. John's Lutheran Church to quilt it. Normally Flo would be part of this quilting group, but they completed the quilt while Flo was away in Florida to surprise her. Flo and Carl displayed the special gift at their anniversary celebration.

Whether a bed quilt is given for the practical purposes of setting up a new home or at the special occasion of a wedding or anniversary, they remain treasured remembrances to mark the importance of home and family. From the Embroidered Doves in Helen's 'hope chest' quilt in the 1920s through Flo's special fiftieth anniversary quilt made in 2008, we have long-standing and tangible evidence that this practice will, no doubt, continue as long as we honor marriage, home, and family with our lovingly made quilt creations.

Anniversary quilt for Aunt Flo and Uncle Carl made by Aunt Flo's dear friend, Lisa Kloepper-2008.

# FOR THE LOVE OF CHILDREN AND GRANDCHILDREN

Probably as old as the practice of giving wedding quilts is the subsequent practice of giving quilts for babies and children who are special to us. Perhaps it's a way to make our hugs go with those children, even when we can't. Perhaps it's a way to stitch our love and prayers into something that can wrap around and comfort the child when we can't be there. It is always a gift of love that can live beyond the physical boundaries of the quilter.

This Bow Tie quilt was made for Glenn Koester (born in 1945, the youngest child and only son of Ella and Bill Koester) by Aunt Selma who was married to Ella's brother, Ernst. Selma and Ernst may have been his baptism sponsors and lived in Percy, Illinois, during those years. This quilt is too large to be a baby quilt, measuring 73" x 83". Glenn doesn't remember when he was given the quilt but estimates that it was when he was a young child. The fabrics seem to be from the late forties or before, including a large variety of blues, dark and light, as well as some brighter colors, colors very indicative of this time period. Most of the fabrics in the three-inch machine-pieced bow tie blocks appear to be sewing or clothing scraps, but some might have also been feed sacks. Selma arranged the fabrics in a very deliberate stripe pattern by fabric and color. She was known as a very good seamstress. The color palette and pattern seem very much in line with its being a 'boy' quilt. The backing is even a light blue. The bow ties all go in one direction, with the exception of one row. It makes you wonder if this was intentional or a mistake, in that by the time the entire row was sewn in

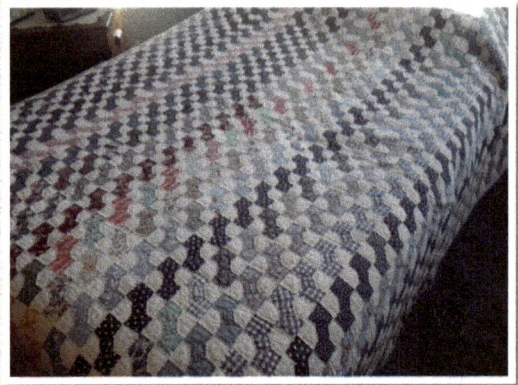
Bow-tie quilt by Aunt Selma.

was too much work to correct. Each piece of the bow tie is quilted 1/4" from the edge. Glenn doesn't remember much about the quilt. It's obvious that it has been used, but doesn't show too much wear or damage, as if he used it for a shorter time. If it had been a confirmation gift it would have been made in the late fifties and these fabrics appear older than that, but as we know, it's not uncommon for women to keep scraps that long. It would, however, be unusual to give a scrap quilt for a confirmation gift, and typically sponsors gave the gift of a personalized hymnal or Bible for confirmation. This is not the only quilt in Glenn's collection, but it is the only 'old' quilt that he has.

This nine-patch quilt was made several decades apart. Donna Buch Wegener (daughter-in-law to Aunt Bernadine Wegener) estimates that the top was probably machine pieced by her mom, Ruth Buch, in the late forties or early fifties from feed sack and sewing scraps and then set aside, probably because she was busy having

Uncle Ernst and Aunt Selma Hartmann—probably church directory photo from the 1970s.

### For the love of children and grandchildren

Nine Patch made by Ruth Buch, reworked for later use.

Detail of nine patch.

children of her own. The nine-patch blocks are just three and a half inches, with each square measuring only an inch. This quilt top waited patiently for a couple of decades until Donna and her mom decided to make it into a baby quilt for Donna's first child, son Randy, when he was born in 1977. They cut down the original top from bed size to make it an appropriate baby quilt size, 39" x 45". Donna used the rest of the top to make matching pillows. Donna's mom was battling cancer at the time they were working on this project and was unable to quilt it herself. She had it quilted by the ladies of Trinity Prairie, her home church and quilt group. Ruth passed away the next year, in 1978. I'm sure when she was a young woman cutting and piecing those tiny one-and-a-half-inch squares, she never imagined that they would one day warm her grandson. What begins as scraps may well end up as an heirloom treasure; regardless of the beginning, the end result is a legacy of love.

Ruth Buch's wedding photo. Ruth Koester married Edwin Buch February 8, 1948 (Ruth was from a different trunk of the Koester family tree).

# Family Threads: A Family Memoir in Quilts

Dutch Boy baby quilt for Flo's son, Doug Zschiegner, 1960.

Detail of Dutch Boy block.

Since the late 1800s, Sunbonnet Sue has been one of the most widely recognized quilt patterns. Some areas of the country called her Dutch Doll, and here we see her less well-known brother, Dutch Boy. While this is the oldest quilt that Aunt Flo has that she worked on, it is not all that old in Sunbonnet Sue terms. This 46" x 67" Dutch Boy quilt was made in Red Bud, Illinois, in 1960 as a baby quilt for Flo's first child, son Doug Zschiegner. It was pieced by her husband Carl's aunt, Kate Kessling. Kate, Flo, and Helen Zschiegner (Carl's mother) all quilted on it together. Since Doug was born long before the advent of the ultrasound technology that gives us a head start on making the appropriate boy or girl quilt, this quilt must have all been put together and quilted after Doug was born on October 12, 1960. I wonder if Flo brought baby Doug along when her mother-in-law and aunt quilted this treasure. I can only imagine the jockeying between grandma and great aunt to get to hold the cherished new baby.

The individual Dutch Boy blocks are 8 ½" x 10" and each boy is hand-appliqued in a different fabric. The blocks were set together by machine and originally the background fabric was light blue but has faded to white over the years. It has obviously been well used and well loved. Carl's aunt, Kate Kessling, was

For the love of children and grandchildren

also the person who gave Flo her first sewing machine, a treadle machine that Flo used for years and years and still has today.

Flo put that sewing machine to good use over the course of raising her family in Red Bud, Illinois during the decades of the 1960s and seventies. She was well known for sewing all manner of clothes for her two children, Doug and Bev, as well as for herself and her husband. It wasn't uncommon for her to make matching accessories to coordinate husband and wife or siblings. Using sewing scraps from clothes that she made for her daughter, Bev, during Bev's growing up, Flo made this quilt for Bev after she graduated from high school in 1980. The fabrics are very representative of the cheerful florals, ginghams, and plaids of the 1960s and seventies. The 12-inch blocks comprise 36 two-inch squares and are set together with white sashing to make a 91" x 103" quilt. Flo machine-pieced and hand-quilted this special remembrance quilt with a polyester batting. I suspect Aunt Hilda helped quilt it, as she often did with Flo's quilts.

Another decade later, Flo made a quilt for Bev's first child, daughter Kelly Gruenwald, in 1991. This time instead of sewing scraps she embroidered pre-stamped eight-inch blocks with nursery rhyme motifs. She set the blocks together with a

Grandma Hartmann with four generations about the time this quilt was made.

L-R: Front row: Hilda (Hartmann) Koester, Johanna Hartmann holding her great grandbabies, Brenda Hornbostel and Doug Zschiegner, Ella (Hartmann) Koester

Top row: Lorene (Koester) Hornostel and Flo (Koester) Zschienger.

Family Threads: A Family Memoir in Quilts

Bev's scrap quilt.

Detail of block.

light pastel pink and used the same for the back. Kelly was about three years old at the time and no longer in a crib, so this quilt is 68" x 86-½" fit just right on her 'big girl bed'. Aunt Hilda helped Flo mark the quilt and they quilted it together. The top portion of the quilt, the pillow fold, is a long piece embroidered with the

Aunt Flo family photo—1978
Carl, Flo, Bev and Doug Zschiegner.

Bev and Doug when they were littler. Flo most likely made Bev's dress.

### For the love of children and grandchildren

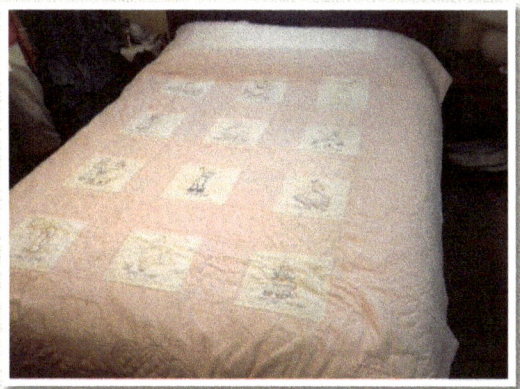

Kelly's nursery rhyme quilt made by her grandmother Flo.

Detail of nursery rhyme block.

words, "Kellie says Read Me a Story". When Kelly was little she always said to her grandma, "Read me a story," so this became part of the quilt. It's obvious that this quilt was well loved by a well-loved little girl.

A few years later, Flo made another embroidered quilt for her four-year-old grandson, Philip Gruenwald, in 1994. This time, however, she designed the embroidery, the blocks, and the overall design of this 78" x 96" quilt herself. Flo used pictures from coloring books as her guide for the Noah's Ark figures and animals. Philip's name is embroidered on the top pillow fold with clouds and rainbows in Noah's Ark fashion. Various animals are quilted into the border as well as a little wave quilt design into the cadet blue border. The 'snow cone' binding is a particularly tricky and unique feature of this quilt. I remember seeing both these quilts in use on Flo's grandchildren's

Aunt Flo and Uncle Carl with their first grandchild, Kelly Gruenwald and Steve and Bev Gruenwald (Flo and Carl's daughter and son-in-law), approximately 1992.

# Family Threads: A Family Memoir in Quilts

Flo made this Noah's Ark quilt for her grandson, Philip Gruenwald—designed by Flo.

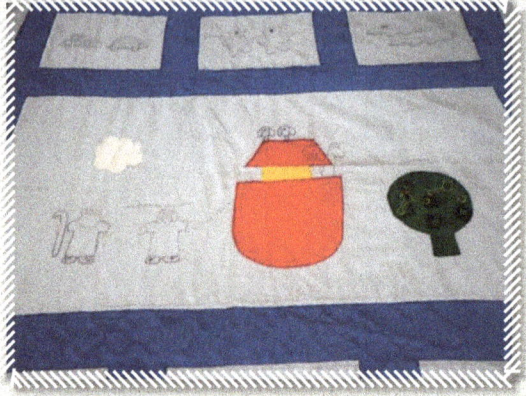

Detail of Noah and his ark.

More detail.

Border detail.

### For the love of children and grandchildren

On the clothesline at the Liefer home place.

Norma's granddaughter Kelly's quilt—Grandmother's Flower Garden from the 1980s or early 90s.

beds when visiting my cousin Bev at their home in the late nineties.

Flo was not the only one in our family to give quilts to her grandchildren. In fact, when I visited Aunt Bernadine to get photographs and stories of her quilts, she had very few quilts left because she had long ago given all of her children and grandchildren all but a handful of her quilts. I know that Ruby has also given all of her children and grandchildren quilts, as had Hilda. Rounding up all the quilts given to children and grandchildren in our family, plus documenting and photographing them, was more than I could manage at the time I was collecting quilts for this project.

Aunt Norma Liefer (the eldest daughter of Bill and Frieda Koester) was not a quilter, but that doesn't mean that her grandchildren didn't receive special quilts from their grandmother. I do remember that Aunt Norma was very good at embroidery and I remember seeing her work on embroidering pillowcases and such. In researching this project, it was my goal to get quilts connected to all of my mother's siblings and I was running into a bit of a stumbling block with Aunt Norma's branch of the family. Since Aunt Norma passed away in 1997, and since I knew she was not a quilter, I was in a bit of a quandary. Norma's son

Norma's grandson Matt's quilt—blue nine patch.

Detail of blue nine patch.

and daughter-in-law, Marlen and Karen Liefer, currently live in the house that Norma and her husband, Elmer Liefer, raised their family in and in which Elmer lived as a child. The house and farm are well over one hundred years old, and I have many fond memories of visiting there as a child and into my young adulthood. I knew that Karen had in her possession a quilt that she had acquired from Aunt Anna's auction. So when I was at her home, I inquired as to whether she knew of anyone in their family having quilts from Norma. After some thought, Karen realized that she did, indeed, have the answer to my search, folded neatly upstairs in her children's old bedrooms.

About a year before Norma passed away, perhaps some time in 1996 or before, Norma laid out all the quilts that she had collected from various sources so that her grandchildren could choose the quilt that they would like as their special remembrance from their grandmother. Each child picked a number from a hat and that was the order that they would go in to pick their quilt. Karen said that she wasn't sure how Norma had acquired all the quilts, but as we looked at the two that she had it seemed that perhaps one was a kit quilt, perhaps ordered from a catalogue and put together by a local quilter who often did that for friends. The other may have been put together in a similar fashion or

For the love of children and grandchildren

Aunt Norma and Uncle Elmer Liefer with their grandchildren, Christmas 1994 or 1995.

bought as a completed top. Both may well have been quilted by the ladies of Norma's church, Trinity Lutheran in Prairie.

This first quilt is a simple blue and white nine-patch quilt, measuring 84" x 88". This appears to be a scrap quilt, but most of the fabrics are repeated throughout the quilt. It is a simple quilt, but very appealing graphically, as most two color nine-patch quilts are. The six-and-a-half-inch blocks were machine pieced but the quilt was hand quilted. It was most likely made during the late 1980s or early nineties. Karen noted that the quilting design on the border was very commonly used by the quilters at Trinity Lutheran, Prairie. Even though this quilt was chosen by Matt Liefer and is officially his, his sister, Kelly ended up using this in her bedroom when she was young because she liked the blue and white.

Kelly Liefer chose this Grandmother's Flower Garden quilt, but she wasn't as fond of the 'girly' colors and didn't use it much. This quilt appears to be a kit quilt as the blocks are all uniform and the fabrics are repeated in a balanced fashion that appears to mimic the scrappy quilts of the past. The fabrics fit very well into my memory of the 'country' fabrics of the late 1980s and early 1990s. Aunt Bernadine also has a kit quilt from this time period. The sisters may have shared the same seamstress in Prairie and even the same catalogue. I suspect that Norma bought this kit and had it made specifically with the plan that one of her granddaughters might choose it. This quilt measures 84" x 84" and is machine pieced. The hand quilting is all one-quarter inch from the seams and is very well done. Karen Liefer keeps these quilts at her farm for her children, Norma's grandchildren. As we took these out to photograph, Karen and I talked about the timelessness of both quilts and the possibility of sharing these same quilts with the next generation of grandchildren in their family when they, too, come to visit the farm. Wrapping a child or grandchild in the hug of a quilt will never go out of fashion.

# ANOTHER VERY SPECIAL GIFT

The gift of a quilt to a child or grandchild is very familiar to us, but sometimes the gift of a bedcovering goes the other direction, from child to parent, for the same reasons of deep love and connection beyond words. This is the case for a special gift given by Uncle Glenn to his mother, Ella Hartmann Koester, in 1965. Glenn was not a quilter but had grown up in the earlier described farmhouse of his mother and father, Ella and Bill Koester. He had seen his mother going to Aunt Hilda's to quilt and his grandmother piecing quilts in their house. Every bed in their house was covered in a quilt.

When he was just 19, Glenn began serving in the Navy. To those of us that he taught to water ski, we remember that he learned to waterski in the Navy, but he took away more than that. From 1964 to 1965 Glenn was stationed in the Philippines, where he made friends with a native whose parents crocheted bedspreads to sell. Even at such a young age Glenn recognized the inherent value of such a beautifully handmade bedcovering. He paid 92 pesos for this crocheted bedspread. At the time the exchange rate was four pesos to the dollar, so this would have cost him a mere 23 dollars, although in 1965 this sum, no doubt, went a lot further than it does today. The individual blocks

Family Threads: A Family Memoir in Quilts

Uncle Glenn home for a visit from the Navy, posing with his nieces and nephews, probably after 1966.

Glenn Koester, 1964.

are six-and-a-half inches square and it has 108 blocks with a delicate fringe edging, made for a full-size bed. It is in almost pristine condition.

Ella became very ill with stomach cancer in 1965. Some relatives (Uncle Glenn thinks it may have been Uncle Ralph Erle and Carl Zschiegner who were responsible, but he didn't know for sure) worked through the Red Cross to get Glenn home from the Philippines to see his mother before she passed away. Glenn brought this beautiful crocheted bedspread as a gift for his mother to give her when he returned home. By the time Glenn reached home, his mother was already very ill, but she immediately displayed the Philippine treasure on the bed in the front room. Glenn remembers that when visitors would come to see her she would direct them to go look at the beautiful bedcovering that Glenn had brought her. Not long after Glenn returned home, on June 30, 1965, Ella passed away at the age of 66. Ella's own mother, Johanna Rowald Hartmann, passed away just a month later.

### Another Very Special Gift

This crocheted bedcovering is not by formal definition a quilt. It does not contain two layers of fabric with batting sandwiched in between and sewn together. It does, however, share many of the same qualities of design and purpose. It certainly has timeless design and artistry. More important, it shares the same emotional connection as many quilts. This was a very special gift that a young man chose for his mother, because he knew it would be something that she would cherish. It still brings out a very strong emotion for Glenn as something that continues to connect him with his mother all these decades later. Don't quilts do exactly the same things? Very often, they cross the barriers of time to share a tangible love for both giver and receiver.

Ella and Bill Koester at their 25th wedding anniversary, 1959.

Candid from same anniversary party.

Family Threads: A Family Memoir in Quilts

Glenn brought this beautiful crocheted bedspread as a gift for his mother to give her when he returned home from the Philippines.

# THE AUNT HILDA QUILTS

For as long as I can remember I knew that Aunt Hilda was the family's matriarchal quilter. As is evidenced by this project, there are many quilters in our family, but Aunt Hilda was "The Quilter," at least from where I was standing down the cousin/great niece line.

Hilda Hartmann Koester was born near Percy, Illinois, on April 2, 1913, the youngest child of Johanna Rowald Hartmann and Christian Hartmann. She was 14 years younger than her oldest sister, my maternal grandmother, Ella Hartmann, and yet they married brothers within a month of each other. Hilda, the youngest in her family, married Walter Koester, the youngest in his family (interesting fact: he, too, was 14 years younger than my maternal grandfather, his brother, William Koester) on July 29, 1934. They lived on and farmed the Koester 'home place' near Evansville, Illinois, not far from my grandparents, Bill and Ella Koester. They were members of St. Peter Lutheran Church in Evansville, Illinois, their entire married life. Aunt Hilda passed away in 2004 at the age of 91, just three months after her beloved Walter. They had three children, Lorene, Leonard, and Floyd and ten grandchildren, as well as great-grandchildren. Each of them have more than one quilt made by Hilda. Hilda's daughter, Lorene Hornbostel, and daughter-in-law, Lois Koester, both became skillful quilters themselves.

Family Threads: A Family Memoir in Quilts

Hilda and her sister, Anna.

I remember Hilda as having an easy smile and a ready hug. She was a steadfast attendee at all family events, and was always happy to see me, as if she didn't have countless great nieces and nephews and grandchildren to remember. I once went to visit at her house in the early 1990s after I began learning to quilt. I think Aunt Flo must have arranged it, but I went alone and regrettably without a camera or recording device. I was overwhelmed as she unfolded such abundance as I'd never experienced of tops and quilts. I had no idea that one person could make so many. She commented on how much she enjoyed piecing tops and that she could get them made so much faster than she could quilt them, resulting in an overflow of tops that needed quilting. I particularly remember an alphabet quilt that she had designed herself.

After Aunt Hilda and Uncle Walter passed away, their family had an auction to disperse the estate, standard procedure in our Southern Illinois area. As they prepared for the auction they counted approximately 75 quilts and gave all the family members a chance to have the quilts they might want. These photographs show the clotheslines full of quilts at the auction. It's hard to comprehend that these were the leftovers. I can only begin to speculate that she must have made hundreds of quilts over the course of her many years, and most of them she gave away. A wide variety of patterns and ages of quilts in these photos demonstrate Hilda's versatile skills that lasted a lifetime. Many

## The Aunt Hilda Quilts

The clothesline full of quilts at Aunt Hilda and Uncle Walter's estate auction. Summer 2005.

More quilts and quilt tops for sale at Hilda and Walter's estate auction. Summer 2005.

people came to this auction to bid on quilts because of Hilda's well-known reputation as such a high-quality quilter. Since I too already had my share of Aunt Hilda quilts, I didn't buy a quilt at this auction. As was anticipated, the prices went higher than my budget could manage. I did, however, pay a competitive 38 dollars for a box of cardboard quilting designs that had been hers. It may seem ridiculous to spend that much money on a box of cardboard, but to me it was far more than a box of cardboard. It felt like I was acquiring a great artist's toolbox. This picture shows just a few of my cardboard and brown-paper treasures.

Uncle Otis and Aunt Bernadine at Aunt Hilda's auction (where she bought a quilt top).

75

## Family Threads: A Family Memoir in Quilts

Around the World quilt top—Aunt Bernadine purchased this at Aunt Hilda's sale.

Cardboard and paper quilting templates, purchased at Aunt Hilda's auction.

Aunt Bernadine was lucky enough to get one of Aunt Hilda's unfinished quilt tops on her auction. Here you can see Aunt Bernadine and Uncle Otis at the auction. This Around the World pattern is a very large quilt top with strong graphic appeal. It was obviously well planned out, and all this without benefit of rotary cutter or quick-strip-piecing methods.

Lorene remembers that when she was growing up her mother did not sew as much as she did when she was older, but would put quilts in a frame in the front room of their farm house where Hilda could close the door and no one would bother the quilt. Hilda's sister, Ella, and other relatives would occasionally come to the house to quilt. This was a common practice that Lorene carried on when she was a single gal before she married in 1959. She, too, would have friends and cousins over to quilt before they all got married and became busy wives and mothers. Lorene shared that when her mother first taught her to quilt she would often make her rip out stitches that were too long and re-do them, saying, "Your husband's toenails will get caught on those big stitches."

Even though Hilda was well versed in making all manner of quilt patterns,

## The Aunt Hilda Quilts

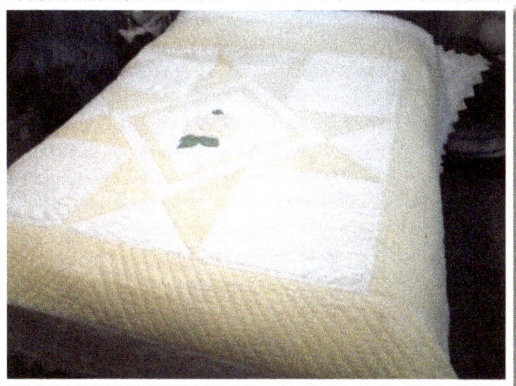

Aunt Flo's yellow rose quilt from Aunt Hilda.

Aunt Ruby's pink rose Aunt Hilda quilt.

there is a type of quilt in our family that is always immediately identified as an Aunt Hilda quilt, the stuffed applique flower quilt, particularly roses. She gave her children and all of my aunts and my mother (her nieces) some version of the applique rose block. I wouldn't be at all surprised if other relatives also have versions of this quilt. For the nieces that could sew and quilt, she made one large Rose Block and let the recipient set the rest of the quilt together and quilt it themselves. Hilda also let her nieces choose the color, thus all of the rose quilts that I've seen are in a different color and have their own unique quilting patterns. Aunt Flo's quilt is yellow, Aunt Ruby's is pink, and my mother's quilt is red. In both Flo and Ruby's quilts the large star pattern is used to highlight the rose in the middle, rather like the center medallion quilts of old. The open corner blocks were used to highlight more intricate quilting designs. The rose block is 17 inches square.

I remember both Aunt Bernadine and Aunt Norma having the rose quilts on their beds when I was young. When I asked Aunt Bernadine about her Aunt Hilda rose quilt, she said that, yes, she had one but had long since worn it out. She noted that with five boys in the house, bedding was in short supply and all was well used. I suspect Aunt Norma's rose quilt met a similar fate.

No one seems to remember exactly when Aunt Hilda was making these applique quilts, but I remember the quilts on my aunts' beds by the 1970s. My mother chose red for her quilt top so I surmise that this might have been in the late 1960s, when she had red décor in her bedroom. By the 1960s, Hilda would have been in her fifties with two of her three children married and on their own and she would have had more time for hand work. Hilda's daughter, Lorene, shared that Hilda loved flowers and her favorite was the rose, which explains why she chose the rose pattern. She also loved handwork so this combination of applique and her favorite flower was ideal for her. Lorene recalled that Hilda often shared patterns with her sister-in-law Helen Koester and they would regularly get together to quilt when Walter was out bowling.

Since Hilda was my mother, Jean's baptismal sponsor, or godmother, she was given more blocks. My mother didn't quilt, so Hilda also set the top together for her, including the time-consuming job of putting on the popular prairie points for the binding. With six roses, the star pattern is altered from the others and also includes a pillow fold section. Regardless of the differences in the individual quilts, it's clear that the roses all came from the same pattern. They are unique from other applique in that the petals and leaves are slightly padded as well as highlighted with thicker, pearlized cotton embroidery. Since my mother was not a quilter and lived in the suburbs of St. Louis at the time without easy access to quilters, and was working full time and taking care of her family, this quilt top had to wait several decades in the far reaches of our linen closet before it would be quilted. Hence, this version of the rose quilt doesn't show the wear that the others do. I retrieved the red rose quilt top from my mother in Denver not long after I moved to St. Louis in 1989. Since I was so near my aunts in Red Bud,

## The Aunt Hilda Quilts

Jean's red rose Aunt Hilda quilt (I own it now).

Detail of the red rose block.

I saw an opportunity to get this quilt completed. Aunt Ruby agreed to quilt it for me and she even let me help mark it for quilting. I think I may have put in a few of my first quilting stitches in this quilt, but I believe that they may have been big enough "to catch a toenail on" so Ruby may have been wise to take them out. Neither of us remembers for sure all these years later.

Roses were not the only flowers that Hilda appliqued. Aunt Bernadine has an appliqued Poinsettia quilt made by Hilda. Six poinsettia flowers grace this cheerful Christmas quilt. Perhaps because it was meant to be used only during the holidays, it too hasn't been worn out as some of the others. It also seems to be made a little later, as evidenced by the Dacron/polyester batting.

Aunt Bernadine's poinsettia quilt from Aunt Hilda.

My mother, Jean, also received a Morning Glory flower quilt from Aunt Hilda. She doesn't remember when she received it or why, but it seems to me it would have been before

Morning Glory quilt by Aunt Hilda, probably made in the early 1970s.

Detail of my Aunt Hilda morning glory quilt.

we moved to Colorado in 1972 or perhaps just after, when Hilda came to Colorado to visit her cousin, Esther Wise. Like the roses and the poinsettias, the morning glories are padded, but that batting is polyester. I took this quilt with me when I went to college at Concordia College in River Forest, Illinois, in 1985. I also used it for my first apartment. Such a unique and fancy quilt in my dorm room regularly brought compliments from college friends. Foolishly, I thought I needed to wash the quilt with the rest of my bedding on a regular basis. Much of the quilting and embroidery has been lost to this harsh process. I learned a valuable lesson the hard way.

Hilda and Walter retired from farming in 1973 and after that Hilda's quilting production really took off, but she was making these applique rose quilts and others at a time when the popularity of quilting in America was at a low point. Ready-made bedding was easily available through department stores and catalogues and home-made things had lost their charm. Notice, too, that most of her quilt tops use solid color fabrics, never any prints. This may have been a design choice, but also may have been due to the lack of quilting cottons available during this time period. Doubleknit and other polyester fabrics had become very popular for sewing clothes but were not appropriate for these fancy quilts. Feed sack prints had given way to paper packaging at the feed supply stores and the yardage required for these large quilts would have been too much for using other, older, scraps. Schrieber's Store in Red Bud always had reliable solid fabrics at a reasonable price. The simplicity of the solid-colored fabric choice lends itself to showing off the intricate quilting designs as well as highlighting the fine work of the applique flowers.

Hilda, like most quilters, was always eager to help other quilters. Flo credits Hilda with teaching her how to quilt, and Hilda quilted on most of the quilts that Flo put in during the 1980s and nineties. Hilda was also fond of using her leftover scraps to make Cathedral Window quilts. She made one for all of her children. The handwork involved in a Cathedral Window quilt is quite a bit more than most quilts. Any quilter would feel accomplished to make one in a lifetime. It's quite remarkable to think that Hilda made several.

Making a quilt is ultimately an act of great generosity and care. It is a giving of self: one's time, energy, creativity, and love that when stitched together with fabric and thread all result in something tangible, long-lasting and beautiful. There's an old saying, "You can't take it with you." Quilters never intend or hope to take their quilts with them. We leave them behind for a purpose. Aunt Hilda inspired many of us to quilt and left a legacy of quilts that will continue to teach

Uncle Walter and Aunt Hilda, at their 70th wedding anniversary in 2001. By that time they were the only living members of their sibling groups (both were the youngest of their siblings.)

Family Threads: A Family Memoir in Quilts

us of her love and generosity. More than that, let's hope these common threads she handed down to us inspire us to live lives of generosity and love, leaving our own unique legacies to be purposefully left behind for the next generations.

L-R: Johanna Hartmann (the mom in this picture—usually called Grandma Hartmann in our circles) Ella Hartmann Koester, Ernst Hartmann, Anna Hartmann Erle and Hilda Hartmann Koester

Since Hilda is wearing the corsage, I suspect this photo might have been from Jeannette's confirmation in 1954, since Hilda was her sponsor.

The same group with Ella and her husband Bill in the front, but this is taken at Bill and Ella's farm in the front yard.

Hilda is wearing a corsage, but Not sure of the event, but it looks like it was taken quite a while after the previous picture. It would have to have been before June of 1965 because Ella and Johanna Hartmann both passed away that summer.

The Hartmann siblings and their spouses, mid-late 1970s.

L-R: Ernst and Selma Hartmann, Anna and Ralph Erle, Hilda and Walter Koester. This is how I remember these aunts and uncles looking.

# INHERITANCES

Some quilts start out as intentional gifts, the Aunt Hilda quilts for example. Others come into our possession at the passing of someone who has left their love behind for us in a quilt. So often when I'm working on a quilt I'll ponder where the life of this particular quilt might lead after it leaves my hands or after I've gone on home to heaven. I wonder if other quilters, particularly the makers of the quilts in this section, ever wondered such a thing.

Aunt Ruby has several quilts in her collection that I have never seen. These quilts are special in their own right because of their design and age, but they have meaning for Ruby for a more significant reason, because of their makers, as is often the case when we inherit a quilt.

This Double Irish Chain was made by Ruby's baptismal sponsor, Lydia Nagel. Lydia's husband, Otto, was brother to Ruby's mother, Frieda Nagel Koester. Lydia (called Aunt Lydie by Ruby) and Otto never had any children. Over the years Ruby was close to her Aunt Lydie and often helped Lydie and Otto as they got older. After Lydie died, her sister, Leona, suggested that Ruby should get this quilt because Ruby had been so very helpful to Lydie, especially when she was older. Ruby commented that she remembered Leona calling her at work (she was cleaning house at Sachleban's at the time) to tell her to come get the quilt after she was finished cleaning just in case her sisters changed their minds. Ruby got a chuckle out of Leona's haste to give her the valued quilt.

Double Irish Chain by Lydia Nagel.

Detail of double Irish Chain.

This quilt is a classic example of a 1930s scrap quilt, made from flour sacks, dress or apron scraps, and muslin. Ruby commented that Aunt Lydie was very frugal and Ruby doubted that she bought any new fabrics for this quilt. Lydie used the classic bubblegum pink, cadet blue, and jadeite green of the 1930s in each block to unify the pattern. Gone are the blacks, turkey reds, and shirtings of the previous decades. The pieced blocks are a treasure trove of fabric design from this time period.

The quilt measures 81" x 81-½", with the main pieced blocks measuring 11 inches. The accuracy is remarkable considering all of these pieces would have been traced from a small cardboard template then cut by hand with a sewing scissors. The rotary cutters and strip-piecing methods that are commonly used today to ensure accuracy and success with this pattern wouldn't be invented for almost another half-century. It is machine pieced and hand quilted with a cotton batting. Each larger blank square is quilted with an identical design that looks very familiar if you've ever sorted through a box of cardboard quilting designs from this era. The pieced blocks are quilted with diagonal lines about an inch apart.

Ruby also inherited two quilts from her mother-in-law, Linda Liefer (b. 1898 d. 1987), who was an avid quilter. After Linda passed away, the family

## Inheritances

*The Linda Liefer quilts.*

divided her quilts and Ruby chose these. Ruby estimated that they were made in the 1930s or early 1940s, but couldn't say for sure, and she assumed by their wear that they were used for everyday bedding. The pastel pinks and blues seem to confirm that time period.

What's particularly interesting about these two quilts is that they are made using the same block pattern but the color placement is opposite in the blocks of the two quilts. What is dark in one quilt is light in the other. Such a simple change that quilters have been using for years affords a dramatic change in look. They are both machine pieced and hand quilted and both are approximately 73-½"x 73-½". The blocks, however, are different sizes, with the block in the quilt with the blue sashing measuring nine and a half inches and the other measuring 12-½". Even though these quilts were made for ordinary use, Linda took the

*A block from the orphan block collection—the same pattern made decades earlier.*

opportunity to express herself and try some different artistic design options. She must have been a very good seamstress as this block seems very difficult and she made quite a few of them for these two quilts.

Also of note regarding this block is that the same block pattern was part of the orphan blocks collection we have from the Hartmann sisters. The

85

The Emil Liefer family
L-R: Ruby and Norbert Liefer, Linda and Emil Liefer, Lorraine Liefer, Elmer and Norma Liefer. Sisters Ruby and Norma Koester married brothers Norbert and Elmer Liefer.

dark navy fabric with a small white design and the light shirting fabric date this block to several decades before the light pastels used by Linda Liefer. It makes one speculate as to whether this intricate block was one that was popular among quilters in this area. It's not a block that we see particularly often these days, as it is very complex and doesn't seem to lend itself to strip-piecing or today's quick construction methods. When researching this block I had difficulty finding a name for it and finally found it identified with the name "Mystery Block" in the book, *5,500 Quilt Block Designs* by Maggie Malone. A photo almost identical to the navy and white block also appeared on page 16 of *Making History; Quilts & Fabric from 1890-1970* by noted quilt historian Barbara Brackman. It was not, however, identified by name in that book.

When I was a child visiting my relatives in the 1970s, I remember Linda Liefer as grandmother to my Liefer cousins and mother-in-law to Aunt Ruby and Aunt Norma. By this time she lived in a little bungalow, very neatly kept, in Red Bud. Her house was on the parade route in town and we would always sit in her front yard to watch the Fireman's Picnic annual parade, a very memorable event in the life of children in Red Bud even today. As a child I had no idea what an accomplished quilter she was, just that she was so nice to us during parade time. Linda was mother to Aunt Ruby's husband, Norbert, and to Aunt Norma's husband, Elmer, and she likely pieced and quilted these quilts while raising Elmer,

Inheritances

Glorified Nine-Patch.

Detail of Glorified Nine-Patch made by Ruth Buch, owned now by her daughter Donna Wegener.

Norbert, and her daughter Lorene on the Liefer home place in rural Prairie, Illinois. This is the same farm where Norma and Elmer raised their family a few decades later and that now Karen and Marlen Liefer live and raised their family. While Karen is not a quilter herself, she has a very nice collection of antique quilts in Linda's former home, including a quilt made by Aunt Anna and the quilts that Norma had made for her grandchildren.

It seems quilts aren't always inherited via formal requests in legal documents but naturally find their way to one whom the quilter loved. Donna Wegener (Bernadine's daughter-in-law) found this Glorified Nine-Patch quilt top in a cedar chest when her mother, Ruth Buch (b. 1925), passed away in 1978. Donna has no idea when it was pieced but remarked that due to illness her mother hadn't been able to sew after the mid-1970s. The feed sacks and sewing scraps seem brighter and more modern than similar scrap quilts of the 1930s. Ruth and her husband, Edwin, were married in 1948, so perhaps she started this as something for her own hope chest or as a project as a new bride in the early 1950s before becoming too busy with her family, as often happens to many quilters. It is very neatly machine pieced, so perhaps she even used a new sewing machine, received as a wedding present. The Glorified Nine-Patch, with its curved edges and geometric design, is a difficult block to master. After Donna discovered it she added a wider, white border in order to make it large enough for her own bed, then had it quilted by St. Peter's Ladies Aid in Evansville in the 1980s. Each block is a 17-inch circle and there are no repeat fabrics. Ruth obviously took great care to make each block unique and set them together in a very appealing formation, coordinating the various blues and reds. Ruth's daughter and the quilt's owner, Donna, was born in 1955 and this seems a time capsule of sorts to document her mother's world at the time near when she was born. It's very fitting that Donna would find it and complete it so many years later.

# THE EMBROIDERED QUILTS

Embroidered quilts are very popular here in Southern Illinois. When researching the topic, however, I discovered that this genre of quilting seems to be the hidden stepchild of the quilt world. There appears to be a general perception that these quilts are somehow less creative and don't display the same amount of work as the patchwork quilts of previous generations. This came as a great surprise to me since these quilts abound in our family as well as throughout our geographic area. These types of embroidered quilts are very common as church, hospital and community fundraisers (see fundraising section) throughout Southern Illinois and the Midwest. Most of us cousins have received an embroidered quilt as a wedding gift (see also the wedding quilt section) from one loved one or another.

Embroidery has been paired with quilting from the beginning of quilting in our country. Historically, it was often used as a way to add a signature to a quilt, as an embellishment to a crazy quilt during the Victorian era, as outline to a 1930s Dresden plate, or for signature and album quilts, but not as the primary design element of the block. The embroidered quilts in this category start with blocks that are pre-stamped with a design to embroider. The variety of designs available is remarkably vast, ranging from nursery rhyme characters to floral designs to traditional quilt patterns reimagined in embroidery. Other pre-stamped products are also available, such as pillow cases (my personal favorite), dresser scarves, table clothes, dish towels, and baby quilts. These products were and continue to be available at Ben Franklin stores or what used to be called the "Five and Dime" type of variety stores. I understand from talking with female friends my age who grew up in other parts of the Midwest during the 1960s and 1970s that most of us learned to use a needle and thread on these types of projects. The quilt blocks usually come in sets of six. Often the package indicates designated color choices for thread. These pre-stamped embroidered blocks and such have been available since the 1920s and thirties. You can't go to an estate auction in our area without seeing piles of embroidered doilies, dresser scarves, pillow cases, and other decorative pieces dating back much farther than the mid-twentieth century. At such auctions, it is much more unusual, however, to find an embroidered quilt of pre-stamped blocks that dates before the 1960s. In our family it seems that the use of pre-stamped embroidered blocks really took off in the 1970s.

By the late 1960s, the use of fabric for feed sacks had all but disappeared, as had the use of homemade aprons. Electric washers and dryers were the norm, and thus the need to protect clothes by wearing aprons had diminished. The 1960s and 1970s saw the introduction and widespread use of the now-infamous doubleknit fabric for sewing clothing. Other no-iron polyesters in clothing and fabric had also become the norm. While these fabrics were ideal for sewing clothing, they did not make good quilting fabric. Doubleknit was too thick for hand quilting or piecing with intricate designs. Polyesters were too thin and slippery to make good quilts. Plus, quilters rely on fabric that will hold a crease, not resist one. On a larger scale, the country's economy was booming and the need to 'make-do' by sewing scrap quilts for the home

## The Embroidered Quilts

Aunt Ruby's embroidered double wedding ring quilt.

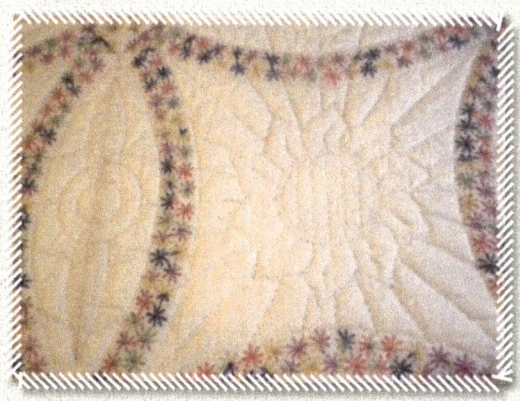

Detail of embroidered Double Wedding Ring.

had also diminished significantly. All of these factors combined to greatly reduce the popularity and making of scrap patchwork quilts. If one did make a bedcovering of scraps during the 1970s, it was often a simple doubleknit comforter of three- or four-inch squares and merely tied, not quilted. This was also the time before the rotary cutter was invented and the big surge of interest in quilting that occurred during and after the Bicentennial celebrations of 1976. On a national level, many women had entered the work place and had no interest in the old-fashioned and time-consuming handwork of quilting. In our family, these were the years that all my aunts were raising their children and busy with the myriad of activities that go along with the school years. Most of them were also actively involved in helping with farming or other work. Certainly there was no time for piecing elaborate quilts.

Pre-stamped embroidery blocks were portable and easy to work on while traveling in the car or wherever one might be waiting. They were also a nice way to rest and still be doing something creative and productive while sitting on the couch in the evenings. These two quilts of Aunt Ruby's show good examples of typical designs of the time. The above quilt has blocks embroidered

Family Threads: A Family Memoir in Quilts

Aunt Ruby's embroidered block star quilt.

in a standard Double Wedding Ring design without all the hassle of piecing all those curved edges. Aunt Ruby used two sets of six blocks to make the overall design with twelve blocks. She's fashioned a triple border out of mint green, yellow, and pink to coordinate with the colors embroidered in the blocks. The solid colors of the border make a nice blank canvas to show off intricate quilting designs. These colors make me think of popular colors of my 1970s childhood. Even though the block design and quilting pattern were predetermined by the stamps on them, it was up to the quilter to choose colors and add borders or sashing to their own liking.

This star quilt is another example from Aunt Ruby's collection. It uses six embroidered blocks and a very common star motif for setting them together. Again, the solid setting fabrics are a wonderful opportunity to display intricate quilting designs chosen by the quilter. I've looked in scores of vintage and current quilt magazines and have never found a published pattern for setting these types of blocks together. I have seen and been told of self-published packets (by use of a copy machine) in recent years at local variety stores, but have never seen anything of widespread availability. Interestingly, however, I have seen quilts set together exactly like this on numerous occasions and not just by my own family members. Whenever I've asked a quilter where they got the pattern they always offhandedly mentioned something along the lines of "oh, I had those templates" or "that's just how you put them together" or "I just measured it", as if all quilters who make these quilts just automatically know how. To me the

## The Embroidered Quilts

Aunt Flo—blue and white embroidered Block and Star.

Detail of embroidered block-Aunt Flo.

piecing of the setting blocks with their triangles and star points looks very complex. I suspect the pattern was shared much like patterns have been shared for generations: one person copied their pattern from another, usually on a trusty piece of cardboard.

The first quilt that Aunt Flo made was an embroidered quilt. Aunt Hilda gave her the embroidery blocks before she got married, so that would have been before 1958. When she was showing it to me she laughed when she revealed that she was still embroidering the blocks when her children were in school a decade or more later. She talked of working on the blocks while waiting in the car during those years. Like most mothers of young children, quilting and handwork wasn't something Flo had much time for. It wasn't that she wasn't sewing; she often made clothes for her family during this time period. In fact, it was during the 1970s that Aunt Flo taught me to sew clothing when I would come for my week in the summer. This was something that I always looked forward to and continued when I went back home. I employed those same sewing skills when I began to quilt years later. Since Aunt Flo was not focused on quilting just yet, these blocks didn't get set together into a quilt and quilted until the early 1990s when Aunt Hilda helped set them together and quilt it with Aunt Flo. In between she did make a myriad of other quilts. If one looks closely, it's possible to notice that the whites in this quilt are different. The whites in the embroidered blocks are much older, by several decades, and have yellowed more than the white in the setting blocks. As with so many embroidered blocks, the solid setting fabrics are yet another opportunity to show off nice quilting. The line motif in the border is a simple way to fill in the space while still looking pretty. It was common practice, as it had been for decades, to use the width of a yardstick for marking this type of pattern.

Aunt Ruby has a little different type of embroidered quilt from the late 1970s. This is one I have seen in the vintage magazines from this time period, although the pattern dates back further than this. These are not pre-stamped embroidered blocks but a block using an embroidery technique on gingham checked fabric called "Chicken Scratch". It uses a double cross stitch in each square with a woven stitch interspersed that gives it a lacy appearance. It reminds me of a giant version of counted cross stitch. Aunt Ruby found this appealing both because it was graphically pleasing, and also because it was handwork she could take with her anywhere, which she often did. Her friend Thea Koester (Ruby's cousin's wife, so only related by marriage) showed her the pattern. This embroidery on gingham was very popular in the 1970s, but most people only made one block into a pillow because of the time-intensiveness of the embroidery. Rarely did someone complete enough blocks to make a whole quilt. This was also the time period when Uncle Norbert was delegate to the Farm Bureau and Ruby would often go along to all-day meetings. These blocks were a good 'take along' project that she could work on in the car or in a hotel room or wherever. Ruby also made pillows for nieces or others (I have one). During this time it was very difficult to find 100% cotton gingham, and in fact it wasn't particularly desirable

# The Embroidered Quilts

Aunt Ruby's Chicken Scratch quilt.

Detail of Chicken Scratch pillow fold.

for most sewing. Many seamstresses were happy to have poly cotton because it didn't shrink or wrinkle. When Ruby finished the blocks and started to put them together into a quilt, she realized that she needed a section for the pillow fold at the top of the quilt. She designed that section herself. Ruby's daughter, Janel Voss, is now the proud owner of this quilt. The blocks themselves are 18 inches square and she finished the quilt with prairie points, also very popular during this period. This was a very time-intensive quilt, probably more so than many

Donna and Aunt Ruby on top of the chicken house—Aunt Ruby was a good sport.

My cousin, Donna Liefer, and I playing on the chicken house roof—summer mid 1970s—oh the joy!

Aunt Bernadine's embroidered blocks and calico.

Detail of Aunt Bernadine's embroidered block.

patchwork quilts. Many of us remember well Aunt Ruby's 'chicken scratch' quilt. Aunt Ruby lived on the farm at this time and had a chicken yard that was one of my favorite childhood memories (and a favorite place to play of many of us cousins I suspect)—perhaps that's why it seemed so appropriate that she would be working on these chicken scratch blocks.

Aunt Bernadine was also working on embroidered quilt blocks during the 1970s and 1980s on her farm near Evansville, Illinois. She would embroider the blocks and have Gloria Salger of neighboring Prairie, Illinois, set them together for her. Gloria did this for many people. I suspect that she did some of this for Aunt Norma, who was also skilled at embroidery and who lived in Prairie at the time. Once the quilts were set together, Aunt Bernadine would have the Ladies Aid quilting group at her church, St. Peter's in Evansville, quilt them for her. Aunt Bernadine was a member of this quilting group so worked on her own quilts as well as countless others.

Her quilt from the late 1970s is set together in a more standard block and sashing style, but uses a blue and green calico that highlights the flowers

## The Embroidered Quilts

Aunt Bernadine—embroidered blocks in star setting with neon pink sashing. I put it on the bed backwards when I took this photo—the pillow fold is at the foot of the bed. Ooops!

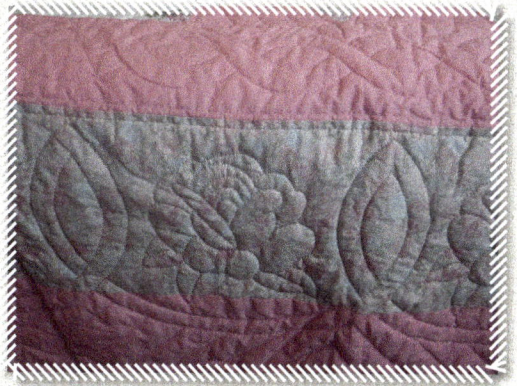

Detail of intricately quilted border—Aunt Bernadine. Note that the rose is quilted in to match the embroidered rose motif in the quilt.

in the embroidered block. These are 18-inch blocks and the quilt is finished with prairie points.

Aunt Bernadine has five sons and nine grandchildren, plus great-grandchildren that I've lost count of. She enjoyed embroidering blocks and made sure that she made enough quilts so that all her children and grandchildren would get one. After they all got to choose their quilts, this one and just a few others were left behind so she had them to share with me. We'd have to go far and wide to document all the quilts she's given.

Another quilt that remains in Aunt Bernadine's collection is this cross stitch rose quilt set together with neon pink and pink floral from the 1980s. The polished cotton floral setting fabric is very representative of this time period. Aunt Bernadine embroidered these blocks and, as was her practice, she had Gloria Salger set them together for her in this standard star pattern and had the Ladies Aid of St. Peter's quilt it for her. Like many embroidered quilts, this quilt has a pillow fold section. In this picture, I'm afraid I put the quilt on the bed upside

Aunt Flo-a different kind of embroidered double wedding ring-last one that Aunt Flo quilted with Aunt Hilda.

Detail of embroidered block.

down, but it does give you a good view of that pillow section that mirrors the star pattern in its design. This use of the pillow fold section on a quilt seems to be most common in the embroidered block quilts. The border on this quilt has a nice rose design quilted in to echo the rose pattern in the embroidered blocks.

Using the pre-stamped embroidered block has not lost any appeal over the years. There seems to be a certain timelessness about these embroidered block quilts. Aunt Flo has also made a version of a Double Wedding Ring quilt in embroidery that dates to the year 2000. Aunt Flo made this for her own use as a "summer spread". It is lighter in color and design for the summer months. She embroidered the 24 16-½-inch blocks while traveling with Uncle Carl. They have always been frequent auto travelers. After hand-embroidering all these blocks, she machine-pieced them together and added prairie points as a finishing touch.

This was the last quilt that Aunt Hilda helped Flo quilt before Hilda moved to a nursing home. Even all these years after Hilda had taught her to quilt, they could still share time together at the quilt frame. What a treasure it is to have this last quilt that they worked on together. Hilda was born in 1913 and

## The Embroidered Quilts

perhaps started sewing and working a needle and thread through those sample quilt blocks by the time she was a young girl in her early teens. That means by the time she worked on this quilt, she had been quilting for some 75 years, quite remarkable. Hilda lived in the nursing home just four more years after she worked on this quilt. Whether the quilt was embroidered or pieced or applique didn't matter, the joy of sharing the quilting with a beloved niece was the important part.

Aunt Flo and her dear Aunt Hilda—at Aunt Bernadine's 50th anniversary celebration in 2001—a special bond between these two.

# QUILTS AND OUR CHURCH

We descend from a very long line of German Lutherans. At least that's my assumption, that they were Lutheran when they emigrated. I mean, who would start as Catholic in Germany and change to Lutheran when they arrived in America? That would make no sense, especially considering the historically strong animosity between the two denominations. I found no indication of religious affiliation when reading the family genealogies, but again, I think the natural assumption is just that, of course, we're Lutheran. Our forefather on the Koester side, Carl Koester, traveled from Rusbend, Germany, to America in 1836. On the Hartmann side, Ernst Rowald emigrated from Prussia (present-day northwestern Germany in the area of Minden) in 1846. Both families located and homesteaded in the Randolph County area of Southern Illinois, where many of our relatives still live, farm, work, raise families, and serve the church today.

While it may seem absurd to young people today, it's only been since the last several decades of the twentieth century that marrying outside one's religion was deemed socially acceptable. Naturally, there was the rare exception to the rule, but it certainly wasn't encouraged. For most people, our relatives included, church was their social circle and very often where one found a spouse. The church provided groups for young people to socialize in their own

The Rev. Max Zschiegner Family, late 1930s
Max and Helen are seated in front. Young
Carl is standing next to his mother

(Carl later married Florence Koester,
aka Aunt Flo).

church as well as between neighboring Lutheran churches. Honestly, this was a very effective means of generating church growth for centuries. Service to church and community has certainly been hard-wired into us for generations.

As was the case with so many Koesters and Hartmanns before her, in 1958 Aunt Flo married a nice Lutheran fella, Carl Zschiegner, who also descended from a long line of Lutherans. Carl's parents, Max and Helen, were Lutheran Church Missouri Synod missionaries to China from 1921 to 1940. They had four sons, all born in China. Carl was born in 1933. The family returned stateside on furlough in 1936 and again in 1939 for Helen to receive surgery. I can only imagine that their time in China is worthy of its own book. Carl's mother, Helen Rathert Zschiegner, was also a quilter. Her daughter-in-law, Flo, has inherited quilts from Helen. Several were made by Helen but there is also the one shown here that was given to the Rev. and Mrs. Max Zschiegner during their missionary years.

This red and white signature quilt was made by the women of Trinity Lutheran Church in Wellsville, New York, as a show of their financial and prayerful support of the Zschiegners. It is dated with the year, 1939, embroidered in red. Many churches and church groups supported LCMS missionaries worldwide and the use of the signature quilt was a popular fundraising effort. These types of signature quilts were also used to raise money for other congregational projects closer to home. In the case of raising money for missionaries, not only did

Red and white signature quilt.

Detail of one of the blocks.

Detail of another block.

it raise money, it provided a tangible item to give to the missionary family for their use in a far-off land. Money was raised with a quilt of this type by charging for the individual signatures or for the entire block. In some cases the church would auction the quilt to the highest bidder to raise more funds. In this case, the church gave the quilt to their missionary family to remind the Zschiegners of this congregation's ongoing support of their missionary work. The Zschiegner family traveled to Wellsville to receive this quilt in person in 1939. The quilt did not, however, make it back to China. Helen and the children stayed behind in 1940 while Max, Sr. went back to China. He died suddenly of illness upon his arrival back in China in January of 1940. Helen would go on to raise their four boys in Red Bud, Illinois.

This striking example of a red and white quilt measures 56-½" x 75", with the individual blocks being 13 and a half inches. It is hand quilted with cream (probably started out as white) thread and embroidered with red embroidery floss. The embroidered blocks are machine-pieced together with red sashing. Each block seems to be sorted by category: Sunday School Teachers, Pastors, Walther League, Families, Friends, etc. Interestingly, on the pastor block there are names of historically significant pastors that were no longer living in 1939 or who were well known to the church at large, not necessarily from that particular church. The name of the famous Lutheran Hour speaker, Walter A. Meier, is embroidered at the center of one block. This is a fascinating piece of LCMS history, clearly demonstrating the congregation's support of missionaries at this time, but also a snapshot of what it meant to be part of the Lutheran church community, particularly in the LCMS, at this time.

According to the Wellsville Daily Reporter of September 13, 1957, Rev. Max Zschiegner, Jr. came to speak at Trinity Lutheran in Wellsville almost 20 years later. He, too, had become an LCMS missionary, but to Japan and not China, which was closed to U.S. missionaries when he graduated from the seminary. He returned to Wellsville with his wife, Taka, and his mother, Helen, to share his missionary stories in a program for the congregation. The article goes on to state that Max, Jr. was nephew to several residents of Wellsville and that his father had been a former resident. This newspaper account gives us some added insight into why this congregation would have gone to so much trouble to make a quilt with all those individually and beautifully embroidered names. Far beyond the financial benefit of more names on the quilt would be the special remembrance that each name might have for a son of the congregation that had gone on to do such important work in the mission field. Even though this quilt did not make it back to China, it surely held special meaning for the Zschiegner family.

## Quilts and our Church

An embroidered quilt that Uncle Glenn bought at fundraising auction for Christ Our Savior.

And another.a And another—he bought them all in different years (he has more at home, I just didn't have time to photograph them all).

The Lutheran Women's Missionary League (LWML) was founded in 1942, but for a century before women had been forming auxiliaries and groups to support their local churches and the church at large. This has certainly been true for the Lutheran churches that our families have been part of, particularly in the case of quilting groups. These groups are typically an offshoot of the individual church's LWML or Ladies' Aid Society. Women would meet once a week at church to quilt for the purpose of raising money for their mission society. Often the groups would take a break in the summer, when their members were needed at home to help with farming or caring for children. Women from the church or community would bring their quilt tops to these groups to be quilted for a fee, usually charged by the yard of thread used. This provided a valuable service for those who did not have the space, time, or desire to hand-quilt an entire quilt, while also raising money for a good cause. Aunt Bernadine, Aunt Ruby, and Aunt Flo have all actively participated in these groups at their own churches, as have other quilters mentioned in these pages. I, too, quilt with the ladies at our church and have made wonderful friends through the process. It would be impossible to show photographs of all the quilts to which the aunts have contributed stitches in this way.

And another.

And another.

Beyond being quilters for hire, sometimes these quilting groups would collectively make a quilt to be donated to a fundraising project, such as the Zschiegner missionary quilt. Various forms of embroidered quilts (similar to the ones shown in the "Embroidered Quilts" section) have been a popular choice for this type of quilt throughout our area over the past decades. Perhaps the labor was more easily divided or the women and their communities just liked this type of quilt. It has certainly been a successful way to raise funds for all manner of worthy causes. Buying one of these quilts at auction is also an important way to contribute to the fundraising efforts. Uncle Glenn is just such a supporter of the church and quilting combined. He has amassed quite an extensive collection of these fundraising auction quilts over the years, particularly in support of the Lutheran high school in Evansville, Illinois, Christ Our Savior Lutheran High School. He has so many that the day we took photos we ran out of time to photograph all of them. Here are six quilts that well represent his collection.

Christ Our Savior Lutheran High School was started in 1999 and Uncle Glenn was instrumental and active in those beginning years, even though his own children were well past the age of attendance. I'm sure he saw it as his

And another.

service to church and community. All of these quilts were made and donated to the school's annual fundraising auction by St. Peter's Lutheran Church Ladies' Aid group. Aunt Bernadine did her part by quilting on all of these quilts. While Glenn could not remember exactly what year each quilt was made and bought, he estimated that all were bought during the decade of 2000 to 2010. He felt that buying these quilts was a good way to give money to the Lutheran high school as well as to preserve these beautiful quilts. The embroidery and hand-quilting on all of them is exquisite.

All of the quilts are of the embroidered quilt style that was described in an earlier section. All are big enough for a queen-size bed and have 16-inch embroidered blocks. Very often they are finished with prairie points. It's interesting to see how each is set together differently. Although some are similar, three being set together with the center star motif, they are each unique in color and quilting. The star pattern, with the embroidered block in the middle, is the one described in the embroidery section as being very common in our area. It seems almost to be the standard for setting together six embroidered blocks. The other three quilts demonstrate their own unique settings that echo similar traditional pieced block patterns but in a larger scale to accommodate the large embroidered blocks. The use of solid color sashing and borders remains the constant design choice even though a plethora of patterned quilt fabric is available now. It seems the solid colors highlight the color and design of the quilting and embroidery more effectively than would a busy print.

About ninety miles north of the school that Uncle Glenn has been supporting in Evansville, our family has also been involved with our local Lutheran high school where our children attend, Christ Our Rock Lutheran High School in Centralia, Illinois. For the 2014 fundraising auction, I donated a king-size Broken Star Log Cabin quilt that I pieced and the ladies from our church, Trinity Lutheran in Hoffman, Illinois quilted for me. We were happy that it brought a good price.

Our family has long known that there are many ways to give and serve. Quilting and quilts provide just such an opportunity.

Log cabin quilt I made for Christ Our Rock Lutheran High School (where my children attended) fundraising auction.

# QUILTING HEYDAY OF THE 1980s AND 1990s

Many of the quilts documented here were gifts to show love and support between family members. Certainly nothing unique to our family, this has been common practice for the giving and receiving of quilts for centuries. To give a quilt is not, however, the only reason we make them. We also make them to enhance our homes and to express our own creative spirit. We may be a family derived from farmers, but dare I say, we are also a family filled with artists, people who create beautiful works.

After the country's Bicentennial celebration in 1976, quilting saw an unprecedented national explosion of popularity. Tools like the rotary cutter, mats, and rulers appeared on the market to entice many a busy woman to consider a speedier option for cutting fabric. Because of the upswing in demand, fabric companies responded by offering more variety in quilting cottons. Fabric and tools were not the only products to benefit from this 1970s quilting surge. Quilt batting also started appearing in various lofts and choice of materials. Polyester (or sometimes called Dacron) high-loft batting was very popular during the last decades of the twentieth century, starting in the 1970s. It was durable, a needle slid easily through it, and not nearly so much quilting was required to keep it in place. All this and the high-loft batting made a quilt look more like the popular store-bought comforters and not so much like the old-fashioned quilts of the Depression era.

Bicentennial Parade—Red Bud, Illinois, summer 1976.

I don't think quilting ever really went out of "fashion" in our family or our area. While there was never a shortage of quilts in our homes, at our weddings or baby showers, quilting was no longer something that every young girl learned in order to complete quilts for her hope chest. However during the 1980s and nineties, along with the rest of the country, some of our aunts were demonstrating a new-found enthusiasm for quilting. I think they may have been experiencing a phenomenon that many women encounter in the decades after their children are grown. The daily demands of raising children have eased, yet we still have plenty of energy, particularly creative energy, and for some women that gets channeled into quilt-making. We saw this with Aunt Hilda in the 1960s with her appliqued rose quilts and the plethora of quilts she made in the following decades. In the 1980s and ninties we see this with Aunt Flo, Aunt Ruby, and Aunt Bernadine. Many of the quilts that the aunts made during this time period were given away, and while some are documented here, many are in the possession of those to whom they were given and outside of my easy reach. Thankfully, they kept a few of their

## Quilting Heyday of the 1980s & 90s

Sewing with my "helper", daughter Anna—she was about a year old, so it would have been about the year 2000.

favorite quilts for their own homes and I have the opportunity to document them here.

I have found a similar phenomenon to be true of my own quilting as I enter my fifties. When my children were little, my quilts were little. I made baby quilts and wall hangings to decorate my home. Every few years I might complete a bed-sized quilt, such as when my children grew out of their cribs and into a 'big kid' bed. Usually I could only sew in short spurts while the children were entertained playing with bits of fabric or after they went to bed. Now that my children are teenagers, and don't need such close supervision and aren't so dependent on me in physical ways, my time and creative energy has been freed up to make larger quilts. Making a quilt takes an abundance of time and patience, something that mothers with growing families don't always have in ready supply. I suspect that this surge of quilting energy once children aren't so demanding has been the case for many of our foremothers.

Aunt Flo's quilt with the built-in dust ruffle.

The first quilt highlighted here was made by Aunt Flo in 1988 with Aunt

Hilda's help, as were many of Aunt Flo's quilts. The two-color design of cream and dusty blue calico makes a strong graphic statement in its simple design. These colors are very representative of the popular "country" colors of this time period. The main blocks are 11 inches and alternate in color with the blocks set together on point. Aunt Flo made this for her own bed and continues to use it today. By 1988 both her children were grown and on their own, and her first grandchild was born in August of that year. The most unique feature of this quilt is its nine-inch ruffle that hangs down to cover the bed frame. Flo wanted this to look more like a bedspread than a traditional quilt, so she used the high-loft batting and added the ruffle. The ruffle also makes it unnecessary to use a dust ruffle. The quilt measures 81" x 95" and was machine pieced and hand quilted. I recognize the quilting pattern in the borders as one that I also have in my collection. It continues to be a popular choice for use in wider borders. Modern batting, whether cotton or polyester, is made such that quilters no longer need to quilt so close together and can leave several inches of open spaces in their designs. The elongated ruffle gives this quilt a very elegant look.

Aunt Ruby has made more quilts than any of us can count, but this is probably the crowning gem of her collection, the Cathedral Window Quilt. Although Aunt Ruby would never brag on it herself, I know she is rightfully proud of this remarkable quilt. Throughout the 1980s, she hand-pieced each of these three-and-a-half-inch blocks to complete the 94" x 112" quilt.

Interestingly, Ruby remembers that Aunt Anna had made one of these uniquely constructed quilts and had shown her how to make one. Aunt Anna wasn't known as an active quilter during these years, so it's curious that she had made a Cathedral Window and taught Aunt Ruby to make one. I've never seen Aunt Anna's version of this quilt and I am sad to report that I have no idea what

## Quilting Heyday of the 1980s & 90s

The whole quilt.

Detail of Aunt Ruby's Cathedral Window quilt.

has become of it. While the pattern may have been from the 1950s (or even by some reports as early as the 1930s), this Cathedral Window pattern appears to have gained a heightened popularity in the 1970s. This pattern seems an ideal choice for using up wildly colored sewing scraps from the 1970s that in larger pieces would not have been very appealing. In this smaller setting, however, the bright colors of the 1970s make for a more colorful cathedral 'window'.

During the mid-1980s, Uncle Norbert was a delegate to the Farm Bureau conventions and Ruby would travel to meetings with him. She often worked on these blocks during the Farm Bureau travels as well as on other trips. She liked that these blocks were portable and she could work on them anywhere. It was especially nice to have handwork for long car trips while staying in a hotel. There's no way to know all the sights these blocks

Aunt Ruby and Uncle Norbert at their daughter Donna's wedding in 1990—about the time she was making so many quilts; this was a very prolific time for her.

have seen. Ruby can't remember exactly how many years it took her to complete this masterpiece, but I certainly remember her working on these curious blocks.

Each block starts out with an eight-inch white block that is folded, then hand-sewn, and then the colored piece stitched into the middle until the block ends up at its final three-and-a-half-inch size. Once each block is finished, it is hand-sewn to the next block. The colorful scraps are meant to mimic the look of a stained glass window inside each square. Ruby used an incredibly wide variety of sewing scraps from decades of sewing for her family. When her friends discovered that she was working on this special quilt, they would donate their sewing scraps to her collection. There is no batting, but because of the folded fabric and hand-sewn construction, the quilt itself is very heavy. While Aunt Ruby likes to display this on her bed when she hosts special occasions, she has never actually slept under it due to its weight.

Aunt Bernadine's lone star quilt (from a quilt kit).

Quilt kits have been available by mail order since the 1930s from a wide variety of sources. Precut fabrics were especially useful before the rotary cutter was invented, but even in the 1980s, the mail order quilt kit was a popular way to accomplish a more complex quilt pattern. During the late 1980s, Aunt Bernadine ordered this Lone Star quilt kit from a catalogue. She had her friend, Gloria Salger, from Prairie, Illinois, piece it for her. Gloria did this for many people. Aunt Bernadine quilted it with the ladies at St. Peter's Lutheran Church in Evansville. Not only is the Lone Star design pretty in this quilt, all the hand-quilting is

Aunt Ruby's flying geese quilt.

Detail of flying geese quilt.

quite lovely. The polyester, high-loft batting makes the hand-quilting stand out all the more. Bernadine's daughter-in-law, Donna, has a similar Lone Star quilt in a different color option that Bernadine gave her. This queen-size quilt was one of the ones left over after all of Bernadine's children and grandchildren had their pick of quilts. If this was left over, imagine how pretty the others were.

As is standard practice in our area, Aunt Ruby, and Uncle Norbert moved from their farm in rural Prairie, Illinois, by switching homes with their son, Ronnie, and his family and into the neighboring town of Red Bud in 1987. By this time and into the 1990s, three of Ruby's four children were married. Norbert was still farming, but her days of contending with chickens, farm chores, and garden were past. She was enjoying being a grandma to her burgeoning tribe of grandchildren and living in town where she could make a quick trip to the grocery store in a matter of minutes. She and Norbert were healthy and full of energy. These were indeed golden years. They were also very creative years for Aunt Ruby. These were years when Aunt Ruby always had a quilt in her frame in the basement during the winter and she pieced quilt tops in the extra bedroom upstairs throughout the year. She rarely bought new fabric except for sash-

Aunt Ruby's Around the World quilt.

My son, Joel, putting this quilt to good napping use circa 2001 (he was probably 4 years old).

ing, borders, and backing, as many of her friends would give Ruby their sewing scraps knowing that she was busily making scrap quilts. She says that she still has plenty of scraps and has no need to buy new yardage for making quilts.

This Flying Geese quilt is one of the quilts she made during her prolific years of the 1990s. It measures 75" x 94", with individual blocks being 3"x6". There isn't much of a story to this quilt. Ruby says she just wanted to try making this block pattern and use up scraps at the same time. She set these flying geese blocks together in sections of matching fabrics rather than randomly. She used long, vertical rows of white sashing and then gave it a green print border. Once this flying geese pattern was out of her system, she says she was done with it. She commented that now that she has made it, she has no desire to make all those flying geese blocks ever again. Ruby also made many Log Cabin quilts during this time period, but gave all of them away. (My Log Cabin quilt from Aunt Ruby is documented in the Wedding Quilt section). The Flying Geese pattern was indeed good for using up smaller scraps.

The next quilt in the gallery of Aunt Ruby's 1990s quilts is this 87" x 97"

Aunt Ruby's Postage Stamp quilt.

Detail of Postage Stamp quilt.

Trip Around the World quilt. Once again, this is an example of quilt that she made because she liked the pattern and wanted to try it while using up her extensive collection of sewing scraps. Even though the rotary cutter and mat was widely used at this time, as was strip set piecing techniques, Aunt Ruby did not use these methods. She used a two-and-a-half-inch cardboard square to trace each fabric square and cut them using her trusty sewing scissors. To piece the quilt, she started in the center and worked her way out. I can't imagine how difficult keeping track of where all the pieces should go to make this pattern must have been. She hand-quilted it with white thread and a straight line through the squares, a low-loft polyester batting and white sheeting for the backing. One of the design elements that Aunt Ruby is very good at is using darks, lights, and mediums to good effect. This quilt is a good example of her good eye for composition using whatever fabrics she had on hand.

Postage Stamp quilts can be found throughout the history of quilt making. Traditionally, this no-pattern pattern has been a way to use up small scraps. Ruby actually made four of these quilts, which is hard to imagine, so that each of her children could have one. As with most quilters who make a Postage Stamp quilt, she started the project as a way to use up scraps. Ruby enjoyed having handwork that she could carry with her to keep her hands busy while she volunteered at the hospital gift shop and other places. Once the sections got larger she worked on it at home. Each square is exactly one inch, with the entire quilt measuring 78" x 88". Aunt Ruby hand-pieced and hand-quilted all 6,864 pieces in this remarkable quilt. Multiply that by the four quilts like this that she made and it boggles the mind to think of all those pieces, all their sources, and all that they've seen.

Aunt Flo was also busy quilting in the 1990s and many of her quilts of this time period have been documented under different sections, particularly wedding and grandchildren. This quilt, made in 1994, is one of the rare quilts she made for herself. Sampler quilts have long been a staple of the quilter's artistic repertoire and have taken many forms. This sampler used a little different approach than the standard pieced-block variety of

Aunt Flo's quilt-as-you-go sampler of quilting patterns.

Detail of block.

Detail of another block—each one was different.

sampler. It is a sampler of quilting designs, not pieced blocks. Even more unique is its construction. Each 12-inch block is quilted first in a lap hoop or frame, then machine-pieced together with the raw edges facing to the top. The narrow sashing is then laid over the top of the seams and hand-appliqued into place. The sashing serves to cover the raw edges as well as provide a pretty design element. Eight rows of six blocks each produced a total of 48 blocks, each with a different quilting design. The back is solid yellow with no need of the sashing because there were no raw edges on the back. Thus the back can also be used as the top. This quilt measures 72" x 102". Flo used polyester batting to show off the quilting and a hand-sewn knife edge finished the quilt. Aunt Hilda had made a quilt like this in the early 1990s and shared this idea with Flo. I remember Aunt Hilda showing me her version of this quilt. At the time I remember Hilda commenting that she really liked this type of quilting because she could do the quilting of the individual blocks in a lap frame and didn't have to have a big quilt in a frame taking up space in her house. By this time Hilda and Walter had moved from their farm house to a smaller home on their property, so setting up a quilt frame had become more difficult. Aunt Flo reported that she got many of the quilting designs for this quilt from Aunt Hilda. By this time Flo and Hilda had been sewing together for the better part of four decades. Theirs was quite a remarkable quilting partnership.

# BARN QUILTS
## AN OLD QUILT IDEA FOR THE NEW CENTURY

As the familiar saying goes, "Everything old is new again." This is certainly true in the realm of quilting. In the early days of our nation, the Pennsylvania Dutch colonists painted small patterns on the end of their barns as an homage to their heritage. Since the turn of the twenty-first century we've seen a new movement of painting large quilt blocks on barns, not by the Pennsylvania Dutch but by quilters and quilt lovers across our country. Barn quilts can be found in at least 29 states and bring both beauty and tourism to their rural areas. Maps of barn quilt trails are organized to encourage tourists to come and drive from farm to farm enjoying the barn quilts along the way.

Like so many of the quilts in our family, we have an individual example of a larger trend. Aunt Bernadine's daughter-in-law, Donna Wegener, is part of the barn quilt movement and has created and installed a barn quilt on the Wegener farm. As of May 16, 2014, Donna's barn quilt is the first official barn quilt in Randolph County. Donna attended a meeting of the Randolph County Farm Bureau's Women's Committee where barn quilts were brought up as a possible project for their area. Her response to this initial meeting about the barn quilts is

Family Threads: A Family Memoir in Quilts

Barn quilt on the Wegener farm, 2014.

recorded in an article featuring Donna's barn quilt in the June 19, 2014, edition of the *North County News*. "I was fascinated and told Richard I wanted one of these at our farm and he said it was okay with him." According to the article, the Farm Bureau will graph, draw, and paint the quilt onto aluminum sign board for a fee dependent on the size of the project. The owner is responsible for hanging their barn quilt and the Farm Bureau is in charge of publicizing the barn trail.

It's a win-win situation for everyone, especially the larger community that benefits from these lively barn quilts.

## Barn Quilts— an Old Quilt Idea for the New Century

Surprisingly, Donna is not a quilter herself. Her mother, Ruth Buch, and her mother-in-law, Bernadine Wegener, were both active quilters. Donna owns quilts made by both women that have been documented in this project, so she is definitely an appreciator of quilts. Donna chose the block design by doing research online, a far cry from the days of sharing paper quilt patterns with friends or finding them in the newspaper. According to the *North County News* article, she found this design, called Lori's Star, on a website called Annie's Quilt and Sew. About the pattern she is quoted as saying, "I was looking for a pattern that had a large space in the middle so I could have a W on it. I also wanted a space on the bottom to put Est. 1880, which is when the Wegener family settled here."

The painting process is extensive, involving priming, taping, scraping, and waiting for the high-tech vehicle paint to dry properly over the course of days or weeks. Whether you use fabric and thread or boards and paints, the path to the finished quilt product requires creativity with a large dose of patience and attention to detail. I think of Ella, Anna, and Hilda making those orphan blocks a hundred years earlier and how they may never have imagined finding their block designs on something called the internet or quilt patterns transformed into artwork on the side of a barn for all to enjoy. Regardless of the century in which you live, quilts, barns, family, and longevity are all pieces from the same puzzle of our lives.

# THE QUILTS CONTINUE

A century of thread weaves its way through the pages of this book. Each quilter makes the patterns her own, in ways that reflect her own personality as well as what was available in the time period in which she was quilting. We quilt for different purposes at different times in our lives. I, like my aunts before me, have found my quilting time has increased as my children have grown. When my children were small and my days were filled with diaper changing, food preparation, and cleaning up a myriad of messes, I made small projects. When people asked how I had the time to sew at all I would remark that of all the tasks I might do in a day, sewing a quilt block or a border or whatever piece I was working on, was the only thing I did that would not have to be re-done the next day. Aunt Ruby and Aunt Flo have told me that they didn't make quilts at all while their children were growing up. There was just no time. I suspect my grandmother, Ella, would have said the same. Once my children embarked on their teen years I found that I had more open spaces of time to work on larger quilts. I also have the luxury of a wonderful group of quilters at our church to quilt my large projects for me. It once took me two years to quilt a full-size quilt for my bed, all by myself in the corner of the living room. After that I decided it was best to let our Ladies Aid quilters do the big jobs.

Ever since Aunt Ruby took a box of my sewing scraps and made a beautiful Log Cabin quilt from it, I switched from making clothes to quilts and never turned back. In the late 1990s, while living near Jefferson City, Missouri, I took a continuing education class in the Eleanor Burns "Quilt in a Day" strip-piecing method and found it to be loads of creative fun. Many a small Log Cabin quilt emanated from my sewing machine in those years. While this method is most certainly much faster than Aunt Ruby's method of tracing the various-sized rectangles, I'm still not particularly fast.

I'm embarrassed to admit that I can't remember exactly when I started this particular Log Cabin & Stars quilt. I know it was in 2008 and I'm pretty confident that it must have been in a lull between basketball and track season because my evenings are generally more open during these times. I worked on it on and off for the next four years.

I've been quilting for two decades and I certainly know how to follow formal quilt directions, but I'm often more intrigued by taking the back roads to a finished project, thus this project was not born of a published pattern. Color and pattern spark my imagination so that is usually where my quilts begin. A combination of fabrics lying on my shelf might catch my eye, or a particular block in a magazine inspires me. It's rare that I buy fabric for a quilt all at once, which is why I'm drawn to the scrap quilt. The scrap quilts of my foremothers were made of true scraps, leftovers from aprons, dresses, or feed sacks in pretty patterns; mine are often from pieces I've picked up while browsing the sale table in my favorite fabric shops. Such stray pieces from hither and yon were the seeds of this project.

It's interesting to me how a quilt can be dated based on the colors and design of the fabrics. Since the 1990s, reproduction fabrics have grown in

# The Quilts Continue

My log cabin and stars quilt
(my masterpiece).

popularity. I first noticed the fabrics that were reproductions of the 1930s and forties, but then the Civil War reproduction fabrics caught my eye as did the other more "primitive" prints and colors that reminded me of the "Little House on the Prairie" time period. I found myself using these color schemes in home decorating as well. I like the contrasts of the dark navies, reds, and greens, against the various cream shirtings, golds, and tans. I particularly like the use of the old-fashioned log cabin block with this color scheme. I often wonder if fifty years from now some distant quilter may say of my quilt, "That's soooo early twenty-first century." Like my aunts before me, that wasn't my intention, only the result of using fabrics that were easily available. Since I had been drawn to these colors, there seemed to be a proliferation of them in my fabric "stash" and since log cabin blocks are typically quick and easy, I thought I had a quick quilt idea for a new quilt to replace the one that was showing wear on my bed. In my experience, and contrary to popular quilting book titles, there is no such thing as a "quick" quilt.

Indeed the log cabin blocks went together relatively quickly, but I soon discovered an inherent problem with my non-planning sort of sewing. When I placed the quilt top on the intended bed, it was too small. I could have made more log cabin blocks, but I was running short on dark fabrics, another inherent problem with my no-planning method. I decided to experiment with making a wider border out of the fabrics I already had and using other blocks that I liked.

Sometimes the math of quilting gives me trouble, especially as it relates to making border blocks fit just right. Now I have the answer to that question, but I don't always have the right answer to how to measure my blocks right. Thus the other goal of this border was to make it in such a way that it didn't all

## The Quilts Continue

have to fit perfectly. I had seen examples in books of borders with the stars offset and sparkling only in the corner of the quilts, leaving the intervening spaces to be filled with scrappy pieces that didn't require precision piecing. I often wonder how my quilting foremothers managed the math to make their blocks fit so perfectly. When I look at some of the quilts in the previous pages and the precision piecing executed without all the fancy rulers and rotary cutters we have today, I am always in awe. Even with the aid of videos and magazine directions, I still struggled to get the points on my stars right. Many of them show by their clipped corners what happens when you haven't mastered the perfect seam allowance. Time passed during the tedious construction of all the log cabin blocks and stars.

In the years that I was working on this quilt, an old air hockey table resided on one end of our basement that shared space with both our treadmill and my sewing area. Since the air hockey table's days as provider of recreational competition were mostly in its past, I found it to be a very satisfactory design platform for my quilt blocks. While I walked on the treadmill I would contemplate the blocks laid out and thoughtfully considered their design. Sometimes I would stop walking to rearrange the blocks, other times I just enjoyed looking at them. Still other times, the kids would swipe them to the side to embark in a game of air hockey. This project lived on the table for quite some time.

Like many unplanned trips, this quilting trip had an unexpected detour. While we were away on vacation in July of 2011, our basement was flooded with 22 inches of 'grey' water as a result of a broken pump behind our property. Imagine my distress when we returned home to find all our belongings, including twenty years of sewing paraphernalia, spread across our driveway. The air hockey/design table sat tilted, legless, against the side of the garage. Piles of fabric lay in wet blobs on the concrete next to my sewing machine desk with soggy drawers askew. Where was the jigsaw of the Log cCabin quilt in the making? The imperfect stars and half-square triangle waiting to fill in the gapes? With trepidation, I meekly asked my neighbor, who had been working so diligently on our behalf in our absence, "Have you seen the quilt top that was on the air hockey table?"

"Oh, sure, I folded up all the pieces and put them up in the corner of that back shelf in the garage." No big deal. God bless him. Like a house on stilts, the battered old air hockey table had held the pieces of my quilt top safe above the floodwaters.

Since there were tables and boxes and other drying rubble blocking the way to the said shelf in the garage, I trusted that my unassembled treasure was all there. A month or so later I retrieved the masterpiece-in-the-making from its dusty sanctuary and, sure enough, it was all there, folded in on itself, unharmed and waiting patiently. It would have to wait quite a while longer while we spent several months reassembling the basement to a usable form. Eventually, many months later, the flooded basement made way for a sewing room like I had only dreamed of, with a cutting table, a wall of fabric storage, and even a design wall. The air hockey table was unceremoniously retired from its duties and the quilt pieces ascended to the new design wall.

With stars and such in place, I tested it once again on our bed. As I suspected, this section of border did not make the end product quite wide enough yet. I'd had enough of making stars and was losing my patience with this project so had to think of a quicker solution to adding yet another lane of border. After all this piecing, the simplest option of using one long, six-inch wide strip of fabric seemed boring and most decidedly out of the question. I'd finished a

## The Quilts Continue

baby quilt with two-and-a-half-inch precut strips in a 'piano key' fashion and thought this might be just the way to use up the dark 'logs' or strips I had left over from the center blocks. I added some corner blocks and this was probably the easiest part of the whole quilt. Now it was finished, right? Nope, far from it. This quilt would have to wait a while longer.

Picking up a package of 100% cotton batting at the fabric store was easy, but what about the back? Feeling cheap (this was, after all, supposed to be a quilt to use up fabric from my stash) I balked at buying any more fabric to complete this project. I returned to my newly organized fabric shelves for a solution. I would cut 12-inch blocks of various light-colored fabrics to piece my own extra-wide backing. It would be like a checkerboard quilt on the back of a quilt. Naturally, this took longer than expected, too, but it was worth the time and effort.

Some time ago my friend, Val Smith, mentioned that since her mother Hilda Nottmeyer's death she been going through her sewing items, including decades worth of cardboard quilting stencils. Would l like some of them? What a ridiculous question. Of course I'd like any of them that she'd like to share. Little did I realize that she meant to give me boxes full of stencils, some more useful than others, but all a treasure. Since I had come to know Hilda through our Ladies Aid quilting group at church before she went on to heaven, it seemed most appropriate that I should use her designs to mark my quilt that her friends in our ladies group from church would quilt for me. First I had to sort through the extensive cardboard stencil archive. Hilda had been known as an expert at marking quilts. The actual marking of the quilt would take me several days of hour-long sessions bent over the table or floor. Hilda would have completed it much faster than I. This is my least favorite part of the process, but necessary. There was nothing quick about getting this quilt ready for the finale.

Ironically, the fastest part of this quilt in terms of calendar time was the hand-quilting, but only because of the team of my quilting friends from church. If I had tried to hand-quilt this big quilt, 80"x 100", all on my own I'd still be years from the finish line. I think it took about six weeks, as opposed to the first quilt that I made that took me six months to quilt at home. The whole concept of the quilting bee makes perfect sense to me. Not only does it speed the quilting exponentially, but the enjoyment of working together with friends and sharing their stories atop the expanse of a quilt is a valuable bonus. It means a lot to me that their stitches fill this quilt, for those stitches, like all the stitches of my aunts, will be there to remind me of their faith and friendship.

Now that the quilt was home from the quilting it was time to bind and hem it. Once the binding is on, I like hemming a quilt. Although the pins can be dangerous to anyone sitting near me on the couch, the stitching is easy handwork, no blisters or calluses. It's not uncommon for me to stretch out this task longer than need be, like slowing down at the end of a good novel because you'll miss it so much when it's over. Finally, after all this time, by the light of that year's Christmas tree, I put the last stitches in the hem and pulled the quilt up around me and snuggled in to enjoy the moment. Putting the last stitch in a quilt doesn't garner the public adulation of running a long race or winning a hard-fought basketball game, but it still feels more than satisfying. Something has been accomplished, something that will last a long time past my own personal usefulness.

From the time that I started this quilt until I finished it, there have been both births and deaths in our extended family and in our congregation, more

## The Quilts Continue

loads of laundry and meals made than I care to count, numerous semesters of teaching, repeated seasons of soccer, basketball, and track. Tears have been shed, laughter made, and prayers said. During the making of this quilt I completed four auction quilts with the kids at school, made four baby quilts, and three wall hangings. Just because I let this quilt rest for months at a time didn't mean I wasn't quilting. Multiple projects mean multiple creative opportunities. From quilting I have learned that even if it doesn't start out as much, beautiful things need time to germinate. Fireworks are spectacular but their beauty flashes hot and fast, untouchable and fleeting. The foundation of a quilt's beauty lies in its longevity.

Quilting requires unending decisions. Some of them loom large, like which fabric to use or which pattern to make. Others are small, like which needle you like or how long to cut your thread. Some matter more than others, but they all contribute. Our daily lives are the same way, big decisions, like spouses and jobs, or little decisions, like breakfast cereal and parking spots; they all contribute in some way or another whether we notice them or not.

For all the twists and turns and long stretches of this quilt's trip so far, even more remarkable is the knowledge that in the life of this quilt, as in the life of all the quilts in this book, being finished is just the beginning. Right now it lives on our bed, keeping my husband and me snug and warm for many winters to come. It will wrinkle and fade with washing and wear and after a while start to have a different look than it does today, just like its maker. At some point this masterpiece will be replaced on our bed by another product of my quilting imagination and fabric collection. Then it will rest next to my other quilts in a closet or be displayed on a quilt stand. New stories unknown to me await this quilt. Long after I have moved on to heaven, I pray it will wrap my grandchildren's children in a hug that only the fabrics and threads I have left for them can give. Time is immaterial. This quilt, like the other quilts in this book's collection, will wait patiently to share the love that has been quilted into it with a very long line of family threads.

# THE CAST OF QUILTERS

## The Hartmanns

**Grandma & Grandpa Hartmann**
Christian born Nov 7, 1870, died May 21, 1948
*Johanna (Rowald)* Born Dec 2, 1874
                       Died July 26, 1965

*Ella*
   Born Nov 21, 1899
   Died June 30, 1965
   Married William Koester, June 1, 1934

*Anna*
   Born Jan 23, 1904
   Died Aug 21, 1991
   Married Ralph Erle, June 22, 1930

*Ernst*
   Married **Selma**, Aug 12, 1928

*Hilda*
   Born Apr 2, 1913
   Died Aug 31, 2004
   Married Walter Koester, July 29, 1934

## The Koesters

**William Koester**
  Born Dec 15, 1894
  Died Dec 22, 1979
Married **Freida Nagel**, Oct 24, 1920
  Born Feb 5, 1898
  Died May 5, 1933

*Norma*
  Born Jan 23, 1926
  Died Jan 2, 1997
  Married Elmer Liefer, Oct. 28, 1951

*Bernadine*
  Born Apr 19, 1929
  Married Otis Wegener, June 6, 1951

*Ruby*
  Born Apr 11, 1933
  Married Norbert Liefer, May 4, 1952

**Married Ella Hartmann, June 1, 1934**

*Florence (Flo)*
  Born Nov 6, 1938
  Married Carl Zschiegner, May 11, 1958

*Jeanette (Jean)*
  Born June 24, 1941
  Married Tom McLaughlin, Sept 7, 1963

*Glenn*
  Born April 28, 1945
  Married Mary Haase, July 18, 1970

## Grandma & Grandpa Koester

Carl born Mar 8, 1864, died Jan 22, 1949

**Wilhemina** *(Dierks)*
  Born Mar 30, 1867
  Died May 24, 1951

## Nagel Aunts

**Lydia Nagel**
  Sister-in-law to Frieda Nagel, married to Frieda's brother. Sponsor to Ruby. Lydia didn't have any children of her own.

**Bertha Nagel Koester**
  Born Oct 13, 1891
  Died Nov 4, 1971
  Married to Charles Koester, Aug 2, 1914
  *Bertha and Charlie cared for Ruby as an infant after her mother died until her father.*

## Mothers-in-law

**Linda Liefer**
  Born 1898, Died 1987
  Mother-in-law to both Ruby and Norma.

**Helen Rathert Zschiegener**
  Born
  Married to Max Zschiegner in 1921
  She and her husband served as missionaries in China from 1924-1942.

## Others

**Ruth Buch**
  Born Mar 21, 1925
  Died Apr 5, 1978
  Married Edwin Buch, Feb 8, 1948.
  Ruth is Donna Wegener's (Bernadine's daughter-in-law) mother.
  She is also a distant Koester cousin.

**Lisa McLaughlin Krenz**
  Born May 19, 1964
  Married July 1, 1995
  Daughter of Jeannette Koester McLaughlin.

# POSTSCRIPT
## NOW IT'S YOUR TURN

Quilters love templates and patterns. We appreciate clear, concise, and well-organized directions. We like structure, so we can follow it, then deviate from it as the creative spirit moves us. While working on this family quilt history project I had hoped that perhaps I could fashion a template, formed out of my own experiences, for others to follow. As with most of my quilt projects, it started with a small idea, a simple design, then grew and expanded beyond what I ever expected. No, a specific recipe to follow did not emerge, but perhaps a few basic building blocks are in place for readers to start documenting their own family quilts and stories.

Start by looking in your own linen closets and stashed-away trunks. Talk to family members. Next time you have a family event, ask if anyone has any quilts. Then ask if you could come over and take some photos and gather some information. It's that simple. No fancy technology is required to begin, just a telephone and a camera or a combo of both. You'll be surprised at how delighted people are to share their quilts and their stories. I found these photo sessions and information-gathering always took more time than I anticipated, but it was some of the best time I could imagine spending.

Don't rush. Take good notes or record your conversation with an unobtrusive recording device. Using the template provided, you can gather the data regarding the construction of the quilt, but what you'll really want to know is the story. Sometimes it takes a little prodding to get the details of the when, the why, and the who of the quilt, especially if a quilt was made or received decades ago. Be patient. Leave some silence for your person to ponder. Ask about other details to date the quilt: what else the maker was doing at the time, were they married yet, how old any children were, where were they living, where were they working. All those types of questions can jog a person's memory and help place a quilt within a larger personal historical context.

Take a picture of the entire quilt. A clothesline outside on a pleasant day is ideal, but that's not always possible. Outside lighting seems to produce the best results. When you take a photo of the quilt on the floor or on a bed, it's impossible to avoid the distortion caused by perspective, but don't let that stop you. You've recorded the measurements, so that will help you when gauging actual size and shape. Also take up-close photos of individual blocks, borders, backing, binding, interesting quilting, or any writing that may be on the quilt. In this age of digital photography it doesn't cost anything to have more photos than you need. I was fortunate to have a photographer friend, Lori Jansen of Traditions Photography in Carlyle, Illinois, who helped me photograph my quilts. We hung them on a screen device that she uses to put up backdrops for her studio. She was also an enormous help with scanning old photographs and fixing a few software issues. The lesson here: make friends with your local photographer. If there is a quilt shop in your area, they may also have a place to photograph quilts as well as good advice on the process.

Once you get back home with your photographs and documentation, type up your notes or rewrite them so they are readable. My handwriting is atrocious, and the further in time I get away from the actual scribbling, the less likely I am able to translate them. You can also take this opportunity to add anything you remember that didn't get written down or impressions you had from the time you spent talking about the quilt with its owner. Our memories are so fleeting—writing it down will keep them from disappearing into the ether. Save your files on your computer or to a flash drive or both.

Now you have photographs, documentation information, and stories related to the quilt or quilts. What next?

At first I thought I might organize the quilts chronologically by when they were made, and that is a good place to start. What I found, however, was that some decades had more quilts than other decades and the quilts in each decade didn't necessarily fit together very smoothly. For our family, it seemed that some common themes emerged as I collected more quilts. Your family quilts have their own stories, chronology, and patterns, so their own themes and chronology will naturally emerge.

You have photographs, documentation, stories, and some sort of organization. What to do with it all? I must admit, this is where I got stuck. Your options are unlimited. One way to start is with a simple three-ring binder and photo sleeves, and your documentation. You can stop there and be happy that you have the information in one place to share with future generations. You could also make a scrapbook-style book. Many craft stores carry the necessary scrapbooking supplies. If you have more technology skills, you could use a photo book company just as you might for your family vacation photos. There are many brands that offer those services. If you have a graphic designer in your family, they, too, may be able to help you. The point is, just like with any quilt project, you can make it your own to serve your own purposes. I had the good fortune of finding Christine Frank to shepherd me through the publication process.

While no publication template emerged, what did become clear were these basic building blocks:

- Talk
- Photograph
- Document
- Write-Rewrite
- Organize

This is a quilt project, not unlike our other quilts, but the blocks are photographs and stories. As quilters we always begin with the pieces and patterns and make it our own. Starting with a simple nine-patch block one can make a potholder, a table runner, a wall hanging, a baby quilt, a couch throw, or a big king-size bed quilt. Even when the block is the same, no two quilts are ever exactly alike; so, too, this type of documentation project. Like any quilt we make, the final product will be unique to its maker. The importance is in the making and the sharing.

## REFERENCES

Online—The Quilt Index

The **Quilt Index** is a project of the Michigan State University Museum, Matrix, and Quilt Alliance to preserve images and stories about quilt artists, quilts, and quilting activities and then to make this information searchable and freely accessible for research and education. The Index houses tens of thousands of images and stories of artists and quilts from private and public collections around the world.

http://www.quiltindex.org/index.php

This is a great online resource to help you gather information about dating your quilts and learn about quilts and their history.

Print Resource—*Making History: Quilts & Fabric from 1890-1970* by Barbara Brackman

Barbara Brackman is a noted quilt historian and fabric and pattern designer. She has interesting blogs and many other books full of quilt history to help you identify the age of your quilt.

Start with these two sources and they will lead you to others as your interests direct your path.

Family Threads: A Family Memoir in Quilts

## Name of quilt/block design:
## Owner: _____

**Year pieced:** _____  **By whom:** _____

**Year Quilted:** _____  **By whom:** _____

**Where:** _____

**Construction:** _____

**Size of quilt:** _____  **Size of main block:** _____

**Binding type:** _____

**Backing:** _____  **Batting:** _____

**Purpose:** _____

**Fabric description:** _____

**The Story:**